PSYCHIC DEVELOPMENT: BASICS OF WORKING WITH SPIRIT

LEANNE THE BAREFOOT MEDIUM®

Copyright (C) 2012 - Leanne, The Barefoot Medium®
www.thebarefootmedium.com.au

All rights reserved. No part of this publication may be reproduced, distributed, or transmitted or circulated in whole, part or any form or by any means, including photocopying, recording, or other electronic or mechanical methods, or by any information storage and retrieval system, other than that in which it is published without the prior written permission of the publisher, except in the case of very brief quotations embodied in critical reviews and certain other noncommercial uses permitted by copyright law.

To request permissions, contact the publisher at barefootacademy@hotmail.com

Psychic Development: Basics of Working with Spirit
ISBN: 978-0-6455435-1-3
Category: Spiritual Development
First published 2012
2nd Edition published 2012
3rd Edition published 2012
4th Edition published 2022
Edited by Sandra O'Neill
Cover design by Leanne, The Barefoot Medium®
Original image: © The mist of illusion by Kyle Tran on Unsplash

I0079919

ABOUT THE AUTHOR

Leanne, The Barefoot Medium® is an empath, psychic and natural medium who reads for clients all over the world in private and large group settings. As a natural medium, she was born with her spiritual gifts and has connected with, been aware of and communicated with passed over loved ones, Spirit Guides, Angels and Archangels in Spirit since she was a young child. Leanne had various encounters with Spirit as she was growing up, from seeing shadows and sparkling lights in her bedroom at night, feeling as if there were people standing next to her, hearing Spirit walking around her house and just knowing Spirit was present. Being highly sensitive and open to those in the Spirit world connecting with her, Leanne was easily able to sense, feel and see people's passed over loved ones, know how they were feeling before they passed, pick up on physical symptoms and illnesses they experienced as well as know information and facts about their personality and their lives. Leanne see's her role as a medium to be the line of communication between you and Spirit, to bring through evidence to reconnect you with loved ones who have passed in order to bring a sense of peace, healing and love to those on both sides. She also provides people with clarity, insights and guidance about current situations in their lives particularly around love, relationships, career, health, business, finances, life purpose as well as your spiritual path. With her background in education, Leanne also loves to combine her work with Spirit with teaching and inspiring people to develop their intuition and spiritual abilities by sharing the knowledge and wisdom she has gathered along her journey as well as help people to move forward on their own path, manifest positive solutions to everyday concerns and embrace more love, trust and joy as they learn, grow and flourish in all areas of life.

Learn more about Leanne at www.thebarefootmedium.com.au

CONTENTS

INTRODUCTION

We are all placed on this earth in a physical body and many of you may choose to do the work of Spirit whether through healings, tarot, psychic or mediumship readings for others or simply for your own development and therefore become aware that there is much more to life than just a physical body. As you start developing your intuition and spiritual awareness and become in tune with yourself and those around you, you will realise that everything and anything is made up of energy. Our world, our universe and your daily life operates like a big energy-exchange machine. Many of you will be aware that you have a spiritual energy field which surrounds your body, known as your 'aura' or 'subtle bodies', which makes you feel uncomfortable if someone intrudes mentally or physically on your 'personal space'.

The more you develop spiritually and intuitively the more sensitive you become to all the energies that constantly surround you (positive and negative). It becomes important to gain an understanding of and learn some basic techniques to help you care for and maintain your energy bodies and the seven basic chakras that are present in your body to avoid becoming susceptible to any unnecessary emotions/problems or negativity that you may encounter.

This book intends to provide you with an in-depth understanding of the fundamental skills and techniques necessary to begin your journey with Spirit. When I first began my journey with Spirit, I heard many people talking about grounding, cleansing and protecting but spent hours researching what each of these terms meant and how I was supposed to actually do them. As an Empath and Clairsentient, my strongest sense in terms of my work with Spirit is my feelings, both in my physical body and emotionally. While researching how to ground, protect and cleanse, I found that most books or articles talked about visualising, which I did not connect with very strongly.

CHAPTER 1: SPIRITUAL ENERGY

Physics has been telling us for over 50 years that matter as we know it, is actually another form of energy, with molecules being made up of 'particles' which are actually vibrations. Your body is a bundle of vibrating energies. These energy patterns around your physical body are often referred to as the 'aura' or 'subtle bodies'. Everyone and everything including people, animals and plants have an electromagnetic energy field ('aura'), which surrounds the body, every organism or object. Throughout history and across cultures the aura has been depicted in a variety of ways:

- The Native American Headdress symbolised the aura and represented the wearer's wisdom and status in the tribe with more colours representing higher level of spirituality.
- The halo painted over saint's heads represented aspects of the aura and depicted the individual's divinity.
- The monk's tonsure (shaven head) was originally intended to fully expose the crown chakra and the aura around the head to God and cosmic influences.

THE HUMAN AURA

Einstein proved and science knows 'all matter is energy'. So the human aura is simply a three dimensional energy field that surrounds the physical body in all directions. The energy which emanates from the body includes electrical, magnetic, sound, heat, light and electromagnetic fields. From the physical body of a healthy individual, the aura emanates in an egg-shape in all directions around the body to a distance of approximately 1 metre and is sensitive to all that occurs around you. So, your aura acts as your personal radar system by constantly monitoring your surrounding environment and working relentlessly to warn you of any approaching discomfort or danger.

No two human aura's are alike, they may have similarities including sound, light and electromagnetic fields but the strength and intensity will vary from individual to individual. It is a dynamic, living energy which is full of movement and can change colours, its energy patterns and vibrations within seconds. These changes can occur as a result of strong emotional and physical or mental activity, resulting in colour and light fluctuations in the aura. The shape, size, colours and the clarity of the colours provide a visual representation of your physical, emotional, mental and spiritual well being from the past, the present, and the future. So, your aura says more about you than you realise.

ENERGY BODIES

Your 'aura', or spiritual energy field surrounding your body, is made up of seven separate and distinct energetic bodies or layers which exist at different vibrations and frequencies often unseen by the naked, untrained eye. These layers acts as templates for growth and development and can be affected by energy of various types including emotions and thoughts.

PHYSICAL BODY

The physical body is the one that you are most familiar. 'Your body' moves, runs, works and plays, contains the five senses and is where you experience pleasure and pain, emotions and dreams. It reflects exactly what is going on in the body at anytime.

ETHERIC BODY

The etheric body is the thin layer of energy which radiates about 1- 2 inches from your physical body. This layer reflects the health and condition of the physical body and is responsible for helping your body to grow and repair itself. It contains the energy you can tap into to manifest your needs and desires in the physical world.

EMOTIONAL BODY

The emotional body is fluid and extends about 3 inches beyond the physical body. This layer contains your emotions and feelings, the feelings you have towards yourself and provides you with the sense of choice and the ability to transform circumstances so that they are more personally fulfilling. The energy within this layer is often seen as colours, whether vibrant, dull or dark, which reflect your emotional well-being.

MENTAL BODY

The mental body is the layer through which you express your intellect, ideas and thoughts and where ideas from Spirit come into your conscious mind. This layer is directly affected and impacted by your thoughts and how strongly you think them.

ASTRAL BODY

The astral body relates to your feelings and emotions as well as how you feel in relationships to people, objects, places and situations. This layer reflects your ability to communicate your needs and desires. It is the true bridge to the spiritual plane where Spirit Guides, Guardian Angels and Ancestral Beings live, as well as where deceased people continue their existence.

CELESTIAL BODY

The celestial body is where you connect with the emotional level of the spiritual realm. Within this layer, you experience bliss, spiritual ecstasy, unconditional love, divine love, radiate love from your core and interconnectedness. It is also where you meet Angels, Guardian Angels and other ethereal beings of the angelic realm.

CAUSAL BODY

The causal body extends about 1 meter beyond the physical body and contains all the other bodies within it. This layer contains the main Kundalini power that runs up and down the spine and connects all your chakras, carrying energy through the roots of all the chakras. It is within this layer that you experience divine oneness and enlightenment, self-actualisation, acceptance of self and others and surrender to the wisdom of life.

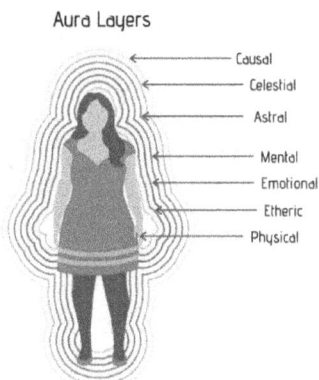

Aura Layers

Causal
Celestial
Astral
Mental
Emotional
Etheric
Physical

ENERGY EXCHANGE

You constantly give off and absorb energy, whether you do this consciously or unconsciously. Every time you come into contact with another person, you are exchanging energy with them, where you give them some of your energy and you may absorb some of the energy they give off. So, the more people you interact with throughout the day, the greater the energy exchange.

The most common way in which you exchange energy is through your thoughts, words and emotions. These thoughts, words and emotions have an energy frequency or vibration which can be low (negative, heavy and dense) or high (positive, light and fine). Every thought you think every word you say, whether self-talk or inner dialogue, is an affirmation. You are continually affirming subconsciously and this flow of affirmations creates situations, relationships, events and circumstances within your life. Emotions are energy-in-motion and are the way in which you express yourself. Because you continuously exchange energy with those you come across, it is important that you become more conscious of the thoughts and words you use as well as more mindful of your emotions.

NEGATIVE ENERGY

Negative thoughts which have a low frequency and heavy vibration include:

- I can't afford
- I'm too busy to
- I need
- It's all my fault that
- I don't like
- I hate
- I shouldn't have
- There's no time to
- I can't
- If only I hadn't
- What if
- I'm not worthy of
- I shouldn't be

- I'm no good at
- I don't deserve to

Some of the negative words people use which have a low frequency and heavy vibration include:

- Bad
- Boring
- Can't
- Dislike
- Don't
- Difficult
- Dumb
- Failure
- Hard
- Horrible
- Lazy
- Limited
- No
- Not
- Old
- Poor
- Scarce
- Should
- Shouldn't
- Unattractive
- Unfair

- Unlucky
- Unsuccessful

Negative emotions have a lower vibration, are dense and heavy, often making you feel stuck, trapped and disconnected. They express an attempt or intention to exclude or strengthen your position at the expense of others. Negative emotions are fuelled by an underlying fear of the unknown, a fear of the actions of others, and a need to control them or stop them to avoid being harmed. Some of the negative emotions include:

- Abuse
- Anger
- Anxiety
- Blame
- Boredom
- Dishonesty
- Doubt
- Fear
- Frustration
- Greed
- Grief
- Guilt
- Hate
- Impatience
- Irrational
- Judgement
- Neediness

- Playing the victim
- Powerlessness
- Pride
- Rage
- Regret
- Righteousness
- Sadness
- Selfishness
- Stress
- Stubbornness
- Unforgiveness

POSITIVE ENERGY

Positive thoughts which have a high frequency and light vibration include:

- I am abundant
- I am worthy
- I love
- I am grateful
- I can
- I am deserving
- I am good at
- I am beautiful
- I am successful
- I have plenty of time
- I am healthy

- I am loved
- I am at peace

The following is a comprehensive list of positive words:

- Abundant
- Accomplished
- Adorable
- Aligned
- Amazing
- Authentic
- Aware
- Blessed
- Calm
- Centered
- Clear
- Confident
- Connected
- Courageous
- Easy
- Enthusiastic
- Fair
- Free
- Fulfilled
- Fun
- Generous
- Healthy

- Helpful
- Honest
- Intelligent
- Kind
- Loving
- Motivated
- Nurturing
- Passionate
- Peaceful
- Reliable
- Satisfied
- Strong
- Successful

Positive emotions express an attempt or an intention to include by taking into consideration all viewpoints, interacting more with others, enjoying making things better. The following are positive emotions that have a higher vibration, are fine and light and make you feel free and connected:

- Accepting
- Calm
- Clarity
- Compassion
- Contentment
- Faith
- Forgiveness

- Gratitude
- Happiness
- Humility
- Inspired
- Interested
- Joyful
- Kindness
- Love
- Patience
- Purity
- Respectful
- Responsible
- Selflessness
- Trust

Often, first impressions that you give and receive reflect the way the aura harmonises in frequency and vibration with other people. For example, if you immediately, 'hit it off' with someone, they are likely to have a frequency and vibration in their aura which is close to yours on a physical, emotional, mental and/or spiritual level. Alternatively, if you take an instant dislike to someone, experience feelings of being uncomfortable or agitated, the frequency and vibration within their aura is likely to be vastly different to yours and your energy fields do not mesh.

ENERGY AND ATTENTION

The belief that energy flows where you place your attention has been recognised for centuries in many cultures. You can learn to adjust and change the frequency and vibration of your aura by gathering and directing energy by will power (intent). By focusing on negative energies you can slow down the vibration, creating sluggishness or stagnation of the aura. However, if you focus on positive energies you can increase the vibration and frequency of your aura.

If you do something because you feel obligated or pressured, or you feel you 'should', or out of guilt, this would result in your energy being low and heavy. However, if you make a decision to do something because you genuinely want to and because it feels good, you would give off positive (high, light) energy. Likewise, if you use negative self-talk or focus on others negative opinions of you, this would result in a lack of self-worth which has a heavy and dark vibration compared to feeling worthy and confident which is a high frequency light energy. When you live your life with love, compassion and forgiveness, grace, joy, integrity, generosity, light and any of the other positive qualities, you will automatically transform the low frequency energies given off by others into higher frequency energy and vibration.

It is important to raise your energetic frequency and vibration before doing any work with Spirit, because those who in the Spirit world have extremely high frequencies and vibrations.

The more you learn to perceive and control where you place your attention the more you can become aware of and control your energy patterns and aura.

ENERGY DISTORTIONS & DRAINING

Because you continuously exchange, are exposed to and often pick- up energy from anything and everything around you, each of your energetic bodies and aura can become distorted and weakened, resulting in you more easily picking up negative energies.

In your day-to-day interactions you can experience healthy or unhealthy exchanges of energy. Exchanges would be considered unhealthy where they intrude on and weaken your aura resulting in your energy being weakened and drained. While no one has the right to take your energy without your permission, in many cases people who leave you feeling drained are using your energies, often without realising it, to supplement their own and avoid having to increase their own energy. If your aura is weak it can result in energy drains or a lot of energy debris. Situations, events and other people are more likely to intrude on your energy resulting in you:

- Being more easily manipulated
- Becoming drained and tired easily
- Feeling like a failure or inferior
- Being influenced to participate in an activity when you really did not want to

- Have strange ideas, thoughts and feelings which have nothing to do with you
- Experiencing physical health problems
- Feeling mentally or emotionally imbalanced
- Walking into an environment and instantly feeling uncomfortable
- Being ineffective in many or all life situations

The aura is also affected or weakened by emotional and mental states – more than most people realise, such as continued stress, emotional trauma, mental disorders or imbalances, upheavals, worry, fear, and other negative emotions and attitudes. Old habits and unresolved resentments leave energy traces in your aura, so it is important to ensure you are emotionally healthy so that your aura is strong and clear. Holding onto negative emotions and spending a large amount of time feeling fearful, jealous or angry, can alter the clarity and colour of your aura.

If prolonged weakness is experienced in your aura, holes and tears (darker spots) can occur. It is important for you to correct any unhealthy exchanges of energy (without saying a word) as you can control whether others share your energy or not.

SEEING & FEELING THE AURA

There are two ways to see the aura, intuitively with the mind's eye/sense/feel and objectively with the physical eyes. Some people have always been able to see auras, without either being trained or consciously trying. Most children are naturally able to perceive and see auras, but they often lose this skill as they mature because they are not often programmed to believe their perceptions are imaginary and unreal so they close down their natural abilities.

The aura can be felt, perceived or sensed by people in various ways:

- as colours (seen or somehow 'felt')
- as textures (sticky, slick, hard, soft, etc.)
- as temperatures (cold, hot, warm, etc.)
- a kind of perception or a "knowingness" (sense something and have no word for it)

The colours, how clear they are as well as where in the aura the colours are located, the size and shape of the aura all provide information about a person's physical, emotional, mental and spiritual well-being.

Because this ability is innate then we just need to remember or 'relearn' how to perceive or perhaps see auras again. Learning to see and sense the aura is very important in developing your psychic abilities as they are both effective for gaining insight.

LEARNING TO SEE THE AURA

Anyone can learn to objectively, physically, see the aura, as it is a natural ability. Physically perceiving the aura often helps keep the 'doubting' aspect of your consciousness out of your way as it provides a more 'tangible' awareness of the subtle energy fields. Auras are commonly viewed by relaxing your eyes and allowing them to get out of focus. You can start retraining yourself to physically see the aura by stimulating your eyes to detect subtle light emanations, strengthening the eye muscles and controlling your vision more. When trying to see an aura, it is important to start by looking for subtle colour impressions rather than solid or vivid colours, to meditate and relax before trying, not to force yourself or to over concentrate because this can block your progress. Don't be discouraged if you don't see much during your initial attempts, be patient with yourself and just keep trying.

LEARNING TO FEEL THE AURA

The conscious mind is usually only aware of what it is focused on, that which is experienced through the five senses of taste, touch, sight, sound and smell. So you can use the intuitive method to view the aura within your mind's eye and/or experience it through the five senses rather than through your physical eyes. Viewing the aura in this way involves learning to relax and visualise either yourself or the other person within your mind and then asking your intuitive self about the energy of the aura. You can start by asking questions such as:

1. What is the primary colour of this person's aura?
2. What other colours are there and where are they most strongly located?
3. What do these colours reflect the energy of this person on physical, emotional, mental and spiritual levels?

Being sensitive to how energy feels and the different tactile sensations that are attributed to energy is a skill that can be developed through repetition and patience. Most healers can feel, 'sense' or perceive the aura and intuitively determine parts of the body where healing is needed. More often than not, these intuitive perceptions of the aura are as close and as accurate as the physical perceptions, if they are interpreted correctly.

AURA EXERCISES

You can develop your ability to see and/or sense the aura by spending time trying one exercise each day at least three times a week. Set no time limit on yourself just try the exercises every day and if you are consistent you should start seeing and experiencing significant results within one or two months.

READING & INTERPRETING THE AURA

It is important when reading the aura for other people to remember that they are opening themselves up to you on a very personal level physically, emotionally, mentally and spiritually. People can be influenced on some very dynamic levels during an aura reading so it is important to remember that energy flows where thoughts go, so don't sow negative seeds, intrude on their free will and be considerate and sensitive with your communication. A few other important things to keep in mind include:

- Be aware of your own energy as sometimes you can combine a colour from your aura with that of someone else's
- Don't judge people based on what you see in their aura – bring up the observations, explain the possibilities and then let the person make their own decisions and choices
- Use your intuition to determine how to communicate the information to the individual appropriately and respectfully
- Remember that auras can change frequently based on emotions and physical or mental activity
- You do not have permission to tune into others energies without their permission – even if you perceive something, you do not have the right to reveal information unless you are invited to do so.

As develop your auric vision, you will begin to see auras around everyone and everything, however you can turn this ability on and off at will.

Note: Only medical doctors are authorized to diagnose, prescribe or recommend treatment. You may offer advice, speak of methods you have heard of that they may wish to explore, but you cannot diagnose or prescribe.

Colour

Colour is a property of light and is an intimate part of our lives which affects and reflects us all. When light is broken down into different wave lengths we end up with different colours. Colours in the aura can be interpreted in many ways and can provide insight into the individual's personality and assess their attitudes, moods, energy patterns, aptitudes, weaknesses and strengths. Colours can also be constructive or destructive, stimulate or depress, repel or attract, male or female in character, positive or negative.

While it is important when reading the human aura to learn to use your own intuition, the following interpretations of what the different colours within the aura mean have been provided as guidelines only. There are many variables to consider and each individual must read and interpreted uniquely.

- **Red:** Circulation, passion, anger, lust, aggression, power, strength, competitive, survival-orientated, active, grounded, realistic, materialistic
- **Orange:** Activity, vitality, new awareness, uplifting, absorbing, inspiring, warmth, creativity, power, courage, joy, outgoing, worry, agitation, control
- **Yellow: Psychic** and spiritual awareness, wisdom, intelligence, learning, mental stimulation, ideas, concepts, lightness, spontaneous, happy, cheerful, playful, fun, childlike, confident, optimistic, hopeful,

organisational skills, discipline, overly critical, deprived of recognition

- **Blue:** Higher mental capabilities, clairaudience, telepathy, calm, quietness, imagination, intuition, truth, honesty, good judgement, seriousness, loneliness, perceptions, wishing, worrying, fearful, domineering, forgetful

- **Green:** Balance, healing abilities, abundance, strength, friendliness, sensitivity, caring, compassion, growth, sympathy, calm, reliability, dependable, open-minded, love

- **Violet and Purple:** Higher self, values, purpose in life, blends the heart and mind, physical and spiritual, warmth, transmutation, independence, intuition, dreams, practicality, worldliness, humanity, spirituality, searching, overbearing, obstacles to overcome, sympathy, feeling misunderstood

- **Pink:** Compassion, unconditional love, joy, comfort, caring, empathy, strong sense of companionship, moodiness, immaturity, truthfulness, new love, new vision

- **Gold:** Purity, spirituality, coming into own power, devotion, harmony, enthusiasm, inspiration, revitalisation, awakening to higher inspiration, protection, solid

- **Black:** Protection, secrets, hidden, burdens, sacrifices, trauma, disease, injury, imbalances, 'holes' or 'gaps' in energy, abuse, drug use, addictions
- **White:** Purity, truth, wisdom, cleansing, purifying, awakening of creativity
- **Grey:** Initiation, unveiling innate abilities, illumination, intuition, physical imbalance, need to leave no task undone, secretive, lone wolf personality

You may also see soft twinkling lights, usually very sparkly and silver, within the aura. These are a sign of great creativity, fertility (often around women who are pregnant or who have just given birth), positive, or a beneficial door will open which is usually dynamic and very positive.

When you are experiencing positive physical health and emotions, the colours within the aura will typically be bright, clear and vibrant. However, negativity will generate darker, muddier, less vibrant colours. Because there is often more than one colour in the aura, each reflecting different aspects, it is extremely important to learn how these interact and the kind of effect combinations can have.

LOCATION

The location of colour in the aura provides additional clues to its significance and how it relates to the person's life. If it appears around the head, it indicates the person's mental approach to the world while above the head reflects a spiritual nature. A person's ability to give and receive is located around the arms and hands, with a clear and free flowing pattern indicating that the person is able to seek and accept assistance when needed as well as freely give help to others when they seek it. Energy appearing over the chest symbolises the person's ability to relate to others, how well they express themselves and whether or not they have empathy and compassion for others. Across the back is symbolic of the past and subconscious, with a muddy or dirty colour in this area indicating the person is carrying old hurts and anger or denying issues causing emotional imbalance. Finally, energy appearing around legs and feet relates to how stable the person's life is and whether they have created a solid foundation on which to stand. If sparse or clogged it indicates the person is not 'grounded' and prone to drift in life.

SIZE & PATTERN

The size and pattern of the aura, whether large, small, absent, or healthy and balanced, also provides you with information, with people generally having one of the following patterns more than the others:

Large Aura: Spread out wide. Easy to lose touch with the inner Self, become overly focused on things outside of self and can indicate the person is feeling very confident. May demonstrate intent to control or dominate others, spreading self too thin and taking too much responsibility for others.

Small/Withdrawn Aura: Often indicates fear on some level making it easy to lose sense of Self, as it shuts down the healthy flow of energy. Might indicate the person is trying to hide, hoping they won't attract attention, holding back their energy until they feel safe to release and allow the energy to flow.

Absent Aura: Person may have unconsciously 'checked- out' and be out of their body as a result of feeling unhappy with life or having been deeply wounded on some level. Temporarily avoiding facing pain or problems. If the energy is above the body, the person is absent, rather than present, in life. Consciously leaving your body once in a while is not generally a problem.

Healthy, Balanced Aura: Extends about an arm's length around the body, making the person aware of others and the world around them, without losing their sense of Self. This supports them in being present and allows for a healthy, balanced flow of energy.

SHAPE

How you respond to life's experiences also affects the shape of your energy system, with your aura generally inclined toward one of the following shapes:

Fuzzy Aura: Can indicate a lack of clear personal boundaries and difficulty defining personal boundaries and saying 'no' to others. The person may tend to take on other people's stuff and get caught up in other people's problems, unconsciously believing 'if you want people to like you, it's not okay to set boundaries'.

Walled-Off Aura: May indicate a defensive attempt to define personal boundaries, putting up psychic walls and blocking out others to feel safe. The person may have a tendency to assert their will through resistance and judgement.

Spiky Aura: Can indicate that the person is feeling threatened and ready for conflict, has been/is deeply wounded. A person with a spiky aura usually has a history of some kind of abuse: physical, sexual, mental, emotional, etc. When a person has this kind of aura, they are reactive and will often hurt other people--even those who may be trying to help.

Healthy, Balanced Aura: A person with a healthy neutral aura has a clear sense of Self and can define healthy boundaries with others. Takes self responsibility, owns personal space without needing to fight or defend and is empowered to respond neutrally.

STRENGTHENING THE AURA

If you are unaware of how extraneous forces can affect you, you can end up with weakness in your own energetic field which may manifest into physical illnesses or mental or emotional imbalances. It is important for you to recognise that your energy field is impinged upon every day and that you work to protect yourself from unwanted intrusions or unhealthy exchanges of energy. The key to protecting your energies lies with ensuring that you have a strong, vitalised and vibrant aura, so that negative, draining and unbalanced energies are deflected. This will allow your energy to be more vibrant and your aura will extend further out from your physical body.

Strengthening and refreshing your aura so that it is clear and vibrant will help you feel alert and vital, increase your energy to do things you need and wish to do as well as help heal your body more quickly and more fully. The stronger and more vibrant your aura is, the less likely you are to pick up negative, draining and unbalanced energies or be affected by outside force. There are many simple ways to cleanse, strengthen and protect the human aura which will be outlined in detail in later chapters.

PHYSICAL HEALTH

The best way to strengthen your aura is to ensure you are in good physical health by:

- Drinking 6-8 glasses of purified or spring water each day
- Getting some exercise every day, whether it is a walk or dancing etc (close to the sea or near a tree is the most beneficial)
- Eating fresh fruit and vegetables, avoiding processed foods and eating less more frequently
- Getting plenty of sleep each night and devoting at least 30 minutes each day to relaxing in a way you enjoy
- Drinking alcohol in moderation Avoiding recreational drugs and tobacco

EMOTIONAL HEALTH

You can also strengthen your aura by ensuring that you are in a positive emotional and mental state by focusing on reducing areas in your life which cause stress, anxiety or uneasiness. Examine the company you keep, if you are in a relationship where you feel you are always 'giving' but your love, time and attention is not returned, it is likely the other person is draining your energy. It is important in order to maintain a healthy and strong aura to break negative patterns in your life.

MEDITATION

Meditation and exercises can further help you to maintain the health and strength of your aura as well as help protect you from unwanted intrusions or unhealthy exchanges of energy. Meditation takes you away from the hustle and bustle of daily life and allows your energy to realign and reconnect in the way that best supports you. Not only is it a great way to relieve stress, meditations can help you develop your awareness of energy allowing you to gain deeper self-awareness, release major personal blocks, and connect with higher spiritual dimensions. It allows your aura to open up to simultaneously receive positive and healing energy, while releasing stagnant and negative energy. Aura meditation ideally compliments energy-based spiritual healing and psychic reading.

MUSIC & CHANTING

Music is a really easy way to balance the aura and keep it healthy and strong. Gregorian chants or classical music are very cleansing to negative energies in your aura or within the environment. Chanting is the process that releases energy that makes the recital of mystical words and sounds mysterious and powerful and is one of the easiest ways to protect the aura, especially if you have problems visualizing. The rhythm of the chant is critical, with 10 to 15 minutes of a particular chant usually being enough to experience its effects. The most powerful mantra you can use is OM which corresponds to the Egyptian Amen, means 'spark of life itself' and is the sound of contact with the divine. When you emphasise and prolong the 'O', you affect others and your own auric field. When the 'M' (humming sound) is prolonged, the entire effect is produced more internally. When you sound the Om, see your limiting and hindering thought-forms being shattered, the energy debris being cleansed and your energies being freed. OM has the power to cleanse, create and release the new so that you can move on to higher expressions of energy. It is also a call to attention which settles and stabilises the aura and aligns the subtle bodies. When you finish with your chanting, you should still hear it echoing within your mind or have a buzzing in the ears to signal that it has effected an energy change.

Note: Not everyone will experience these sensations.

HERBS, INCENSE & ESSENTIAL OILS

Fragrances whether herbs, incense or essential oils, can also be used to protect and strengthen the auric field. Smudging, a Native American tradition is the practice of using the smoke and fragrance of various herbs to cleanse the aura and environment. Fragrances whether incense or essential oils, most strongly affect the aura and energies of an emotional and mental nature and have been used to counter the effects of disease and illness, whether physical, emotional, mental or spiritual. Sage and sweet-grass combination is common for cleansing and balancing the aura. Frankincense has a high energy vibration and is cleansing and protecting to the aura. Gardenia helps prevent healers and counsellors from becoming too entangled in the problems of others and strengthens the aura so that emotional objectivity is maintained.

CRYSTALS

The energy released by various crystals and stones are easily absorbed into the human auric field. A quartz crystal is a great tool for protecting and strengthening the aura. The energy inherent in quartz crystal is excellent for protecting, cleansing, amplifying and strengthening. Double terminators (points and both ends) are extremely effective for strengthening, especially if you know you will be going into tense or draining situations.

ANIMALS

Animals also have auras which affect you and they can help to balance and stabilise your physical, emotional, mental and spiritual energies.

THE CHAKRAS

There are centers of energy physically and spiritually associated with various parts of our bodies, called chakras. The word chakra is derived from the Sanskrit word meaning wheel because they are often seen and/or felt as a wheel of energy which is continuously revolving or rotating. There are seven major chakra points that span all layers of the energy body and connect with your physical body.

WHAT?

The chakra's (energy centers) are points of contact with the aspects of our being that are beyond the physical, but they are also intrinsically linked to the body that we see and feel. The chakras are often represented symbolically as a lotus, with each having a different number of petals with the higher chakras having more petals to indicate their higher frequency and vibration. As energy flows through each of the chakra centers, they are activated and begin to spin or blossom.

WHERE?

The seven major chakras run vertically from the base of your spine to the top of your head and correspond to the points on the body where the major hormonal glands are located. Though fixed in the central spinal column they are located on both the front and back of the body, and work through it. There are also minor chakra points located in the palms of the hands, the soles of the feet, and at major joints in the arms and legs.

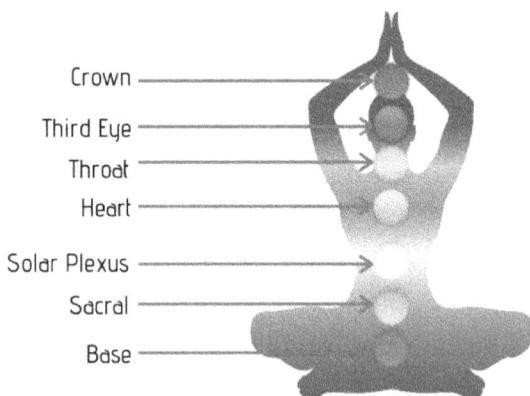

Crown
Third Eye
Throat
Heart
Solar Plexus
Sacral
Base

Base Chakra

The first energy center which is red in colour is the base chakra, located at the base-of-the-spinal column and the pubic bone (between anus and genitals). On a physical level this chakra corresponds to the reproductive organs gonads, adrenal gland, the kidneys and the spinal column. The base energy center holds your basic needs for survival, security and safety. This chakra is powerfully related to your connection with Mother Earth as it is through this center that energy from the earth enters your physical body and helps you to be grounded in the physical world. It is also the center of manifestation where you make things happen in the material world (business or material possessions). The energy to succeed also comes from this chakra. Your life-force (Kundalini) energy is stored in the base chakra and all of the other chakras rely on it to be clear and free-flowing so that the energy can rise and nourish all the chakras. The base chakra governs your perception of the physical world, willpower, motivation and intent and is associated with stability, solidarity, unity, athletic ability, groundedness, survival, sensuality, pleasure and power.

Sacral Chakra

The second chakra is the sacral, located midway between the navel and base of the spine and is orange in colour. The sacral, on a physical level, is associated with the spleen, kidneys and bladder as well as reproductive capacity. It is linked to the emotional body and is where you experience sexual energy and pleasure, creativity, intuition and sense of self-worth as well as your sense of innocence and childlike joy. This chakra governs your confidence in your own creativity, ability to relate to others in an open and friendly way as well as where you experience the deep feelings associated with physical manifestation. It is associated with difference, separation, change, duality and movement.

Solar Plexus Chakra

The solar plexus is the third chakra, located about 5 centimetres below the breastbone in the centre behind the stomach. This chakra is yellow in colour and is associated with the mental body as well as the pancreas, stomach, liver, gall bladder, upper abdomen as well as the nervous system. It plays an important part in your relationship to the world and to people, places, and things within it including your ability to connect, belong and make long term intimate relationships as well as feelings of contentment and trust. Through the solar plexus we experience thoughts, opinions, judgements, transformation and find balance. The solar plexus is the seat of your personal power, the place of the ego, creativity, passions, impulses, anger and strength. It is also associated with astral travel and your openness to connecting with your spirit guides for psychic and spiritual development.

Heart Chakra

The fourth energy center is the heart chakra, located behind the breast bone in front and on the spine between the shoulder blades in back. The heart chakra is green in colour, with a secondary colour of pink for love, and is associated with the astral body, as well as the immune system, heart, blood, circulatory system and the endocrine system. It is the epi center for love, compassion, healing and spirituality acting as a bridge between the physical and spiritual worlds. The heart chakra is the center of love and emotional well-being and holds your ability to love and accept yourself and others unconditionally as well as to give and to receive love.

Throat Chakra

The fifth chakra is the throat which is blue in colour and is located in the V of the collarbone and at the lower neck. This chakra is linked to the etheric body and on the physical level is associated with the throat, lungs, jaw, vocal cords, digestive tract and thyroid gland. It is the center of communication, sound, self-expression, expression of creativity through thought, speech and writing as well as your expression of higher spiritual will. The throat is where anger is stored and finally let go of as well as where the possibility for change, healing and transformation are located.

Third Eye Chakra

The third eye is the sixth chakra which is indigo and located in the center of your brow between the eyebrows. This energy

41

center is linked to the celestial body and physically with the pineal or pituitary gland, hypothalamus, left eye, ears, nose, and the central nervous system. The third eye has control over seeing, not only in the physical sense, but in the spiritual sense. It is where psychic ability, higher intuition, clairvoyance, spiritual insights, wisdom and other forms of knowing as well as the energies of spirit and light come in. Through the power of the sixth chakra, you can receive guidance, channel, and tune into your Higher Self. You can also use the power of this chakra to visualise and see things in your mind's eye to help create new realities for yourself on the physical plane as well as purify negative tendencies and eliminate selfish attitudes.

Crown Chakra

The seventh chakra is referred to as the Crown and is located at the top of the head and is violet/white in colour. It is linked to the pineal gland, upper brain, right eye and serves as the entry point for Universal/Spiritual energy to enter your bodies and then flow through to the other six chakras below. The crown is linked to spirituality, enlightenment, transcendence, consciousness and it is through this energy center that you receive wisdom and the highest guidance. It also influences spiritual will, inspiration, idealism and is our connection with the Universe. There is a silver cord that connects the aura and energy bodies which extends from the crown. Your soul comes into your physical body through the crown at birth and leaves from the crown at death.

Minor Chakra's

There are also 21 'minor' chakras distributed all over the body on the soles of the feet, hands, at the knees, palms of the hands, elbows, groin, clavicles, navel, shoulders and ear. These chakra's are not associated with endocrine glands and so have less of an impact on our physical bodies.

It is important to learn about your energy so that you are not so easily upset or affected by other people's energies, particularly negative energies. It is also important to learn to consciously control your energy field so that you can interact with and adjust to other people's energy fields or the environment as strongly or as weakly as needed. The more you develop the naturally ability to control your energy, through expanding and contracting your aura, the greater control you will have over your own life and environment. The more sensitive you become to your aura, the more you can recognize and control what energies you allow into and out of it. Also, as you develop the ability to see and feel the more subtle aspects of life, you are blessed in other ways. Your intuition unfolds and increases, and the childlike joy and wonder of life returns. Every day becomes an adventure.

Every day becomes a new blessing. Knowing about the aura, universal energy and how it affects the aura, and how to use this energy to heal the aura is a vitally important part of magical healing. Remember, every time you have a strong emotional, mental or spiritual reaction, there is a corresponding change in the aura which may affect the colour, shape etc. The activities you involve yourself in reflect themselves in your aura.

CHAPTER 2. CENTERING

Many spiritual teachers speak about 'getting centered', which means to gather all of your scattered energies into your core - into the centre of your body – so that your energy vibrates at higher frequencies. Centering is the first step in beginning to explore your spiritual gifts and work with Spirit. It involves placing your awareness on your breath and your personal power centre, whether it is your third eye, heart, or solar plexus chakra, whatever feels right for you. When you are centered it allows you to bring your conscious attention back to the present moment in time and bring any scattered energy back into the centre of your body. So when you hear someone talk about 'getting centered', they are saying that you need to 'pull yourself together' spiritually by bringing your attention and energies into the centre of your being.

CONSCIOUS AWARENESS

Consciousness refers to your personal awareness of your own thoughts, memories, feelings, sensations, actions and environment which are constantly shifting and changing. When you are consciously aware you are able to make smooth and effortless choices which can shift your thoughts and emotions from one moment to the next, which in turn have an impact on your experiences.

PAST, PRESENT & FUTURE

When your energy becomes scattered and you are focused on your external needs, you are likely to have slipped into thoughts, emotions and patterns of behaviour which are based on fear. When you are living in fear, you are living in the past, or future and your thoughts, decisions and actions are motivated by fear (eg. fear of death, loneliness, poverty or pain). Some of the common fears you may experience which keep you from being your authentic self include:

- Success
- Being poor
- Speaking up
- Intimacy
- Conflict
- Making decisions
- Failure
- Lack of love
- Losing someone
- Change and uncertainty
- Disappointing others
- Commitment
- Spirit
- Rejection
- Being worthy
- Lack of time
- Loneliness

- Lack of support
- Not getting what you want
- Lack of knowledge

When you are motivated by fear, life seems to be stressful and a constant struggle with a sense of dissatisfaction despite your achievements. You feel insecure and like there is not enough, despite everything you have accomplished and accumulated. When you are living in the past or the future opportunities and experiences also seem to pass you by because you are not in the present moment and passively sit back and let things happen, your insights into your own strengths and weaknesses are impaired resulting in a resistance and lack of courage in facing the real you. When you live in fear there is no real peace or contentment, your emotions and thoughts are numb, resulting in poor decisions and judgments which lead to more fear. When you are sitting in a space of fear, you attract fear-based experiences and more problems into your life. The more fearful you are, the more you feel the need to control everything within your life. Fear can also result in you being paralysed into inaction. So fear is a negative energy which keeps you locked into old habits, beliefs and actions as a way of keeping you in space where you feel comfortable and stops you from learning and growing. If you are fearful of seeing, hearing or sensing Spirits, you will also hold yourself back and stop yourself from moving forward in your spiritual development.

When you gather your attention and energy back into your core, you are living in the present moment and have an internal focus. This allows you to become consciously aware of your thoughts and emotions in the present moment. You can intentionally choose over and over again in each and every moment to be present and concentrate on what is happening around you, without distraction. By being present, you are able to consciously choose to improve your thoughts, attitudes, beliefs and behaviours and learn to fill yourself with positive energies such as joy, pleasure, gratitude, self- esteem and abundance in each moment. When you are present, you will begin to see things which used to cause you frustration such as waiting in line or at traffic lights, as opportunities for practicing being conscious and getting back to your centre and the moment. You also feel free, do not need to control or manipulate events or people and you have a sense of inner peace, serenity and contentment.

AUTHENTIC SELF

Living consciously, requires absolute presence which means being your authentic self. When you are being your authentic self you know and understand yourself, your personality, learned behaviours, values, beliefs, needs, goals and motives. You know what your strengths are, have the courage to acknowledge your limitations, embrace your vulnerability and understand that there are things you can change and things you cannot. When you are living authentically, you live openly and honestly as well as accept and appreciate yourself and allow others to do the same, even if others do not appreciate the real you (body, mind and heart). You are able to reflect on the choices you have made, the events which have taken place and recognise the people who have contributed to who you are. As an authentic person you are congruent and in alignment with your values, beliefs and actions, that is, you do what you say by walking your walk. When you are your authentic self you have the confidence to be humble and feel content, whole, complete and consciously aware of and own who you are and your energy.

LIVING IN INTEGRITY

When you are consciously aware and present, you are able to live your life in integrity by being open and honest with yourself and those around you. If honesty is a challenge for you, it is more than likely that you are not being honest with yourself. When you tell other people lies, even white lies, you are essentially being dishonest with yourself and there are more than likely other areas of your life where you are lying to yourself. The more open and honest you are able to be about your own thoughts and feelings, the more conscious and capable you become of accepting the truth and speaking the truth. So it is important to ensure that the words, thoughts, feelings and actions you choose in each moment are honest and in direct alignment with your core values and for the highest good of all concerned. By being completely open and honest, you are then able to stand fully in your power, from a space of strength, courage and compassion for yourself as well as those around you. Therefore, by living in the present moment and focusing on your internal needs, you are centering your energy and becoming more conscious of what is happening around you so that you can learn, grow and move forward on your journey.

SPEAK YOUR TRUTH

Speaking your truth is an essential aspect of living your life with authenticity and integrity. It is not about sharing your opinions, it is about expressing what you think and feel in a clear, authentic and vulnerable way. When you speak your truth you have the courage to have difficult conversations, even if your voice and legs shake or your heart races, which usually happens when you get authentic and allow yourself to be vulnerable. Your actions are also in direct alignment with your words when you speak your truth, as you are fully embracing and expressing your authentic self. It is important to have the courage to speak up in all areas of your life, whether it is at work, in your relationship, with family and friends or people you come across in your everyday life.

HIGHER PERSPECTIVE

When you become more consciously aware, you are able to see your life and the events, situations, thoughts, perceptions and emotions within it, from a different, higher perspective. Living under the higher perspective, allows you to see things for what they are and fully understand that everything that happens to you is an invitation to rise above and learn and grow. Throughout your everyday life, you may come across people, who are living in fear and their thoughts, emotions and patterns of behaviour are fuelled by their underlying fear which in turn attracts more problems and negative experiences into their lives. It is important for you to become consciously aware in each moment of any fear-based thoughts, emotions and actions which are taking place so that you can take responsibility for viewing them from the higher perspective by asking yourself what is this person or situation teaching me? By doing this, you will be able to identify with what is going on, both externally and internally, and make a conscious choice to become aware of the learning within it and remain calm and peaceful, not allowing the events or people within in to lower your energy. While there may be some events that have an impact and lower your energy for a time, it is important that you are able to detach yourself emotionally, find your center and rise above the situation to find the higher perspective. Remember, in each moment you are able to make a conscious choice and as such can refuse to participate in any thought, emotion or situation that lowers your consciousness into a space of fear.

COMPASSION

One of the most important aspects of becoming more consciously aware is to develop true compassion, the source of unconditional love and connectedness with yourself, others, and all that exists. Having compassion means that you have the ability to understand your own or others emotional state, as well as having the desire to lighten or reduce their pain and distress. When you have compassion, you often also display empathy, which is the ability to put yourself in the other person's shoes. Having compassion or empathy does not mean feeling sorry for yourself or for others or indulging your own or others weaknesses as this only serves to keep you in the victim role. It also does not mean doing for someone else what they can do for themselves as this would not help them gain the learning and knowledge from the situation and therefore not serve their highest good. The best kind of compassion you can show to others is to allow them to experience their emotions without causing them further pain or distress.

Throughout your life you may have also been taught to take a dualistic view of people, events and circumstances, seeing them as good or bad, right or wrong, black or white. However, when you see things in this way, you are in fact judging people or events based on your own underlying values, beliefs and experiences which in turn disconnects you from yourself, others and all that is. The ability to offer compassion, empathy and unconditional love, helps you to understand and see that we are all connected, that there are no dualities and to uplift others so they can realise their full potential. In order to raise your consciousness, it is important to learn to show empathy and compassion and to love everyone and everything, no matter what.

CLARITY

When you are centered, you have clarity which helps you to focus your mind and gives you the power to think and act intelligently. However, when your thoughts lack focus and direction, and you keep thinking, feeling and taking the same actions, you lack clarity and are not centred in the present moment. You can centre yourself again by sitting down and getting clarity about   what you truly desire most and setting goals that you can take positive steps towards achieving.

WHY?

When your energy is 'out' of your body (not centered), you are usually trying to 'get something' in order to satisfy a need from outside of yourself. For example, your energy may be scattered as a result of trying to satisfy your need to be able to express yourself, to be heard and accepted, to be loved, supported and happy. When you get into a space where you are attempting to get something or fulfill a need outside of yourself, you may feel overwhelmed, anxious, stressed, and be filled with doubt and fear. Some of the signs that you may not be centered include:

- Cluttered and unfocused thinking
- Carrying tension within your physical body
- Overeating

- Being stuck in a mental fog and unable to see clearly
- Worrying needlessly about 'what if's'
- Constantly being distracted by trivial issues and thoughts
- Being reactive to events and circumstances instead of proactive
- Seeing and observing things from a negative and inaccurate perspective
- Judging and separating yourself from others (eg. gossiping and talking negatively about people behind their backs)
- Holding onto false beliefs which are disempowering and stop you from moving forward
- Continual negative thoughts and playing out negative emotional patterns because they feel safe and comfortable, even if they are painful
- Feeling as if you are not fully there (eg. the lights are on but no one is home)
- Doing what others tell you to do (eg. doing the right thing by others)
- Feeling powerless to change circumstances in your life

When you become more centered and conscious in the moment, you are able to:

- stay in the present instead of thinking about the past or the future
- make deliberate, intelligent, and mindful decisions

- maintain a positive emotional state regardless of conditions around you
- release and let go of energies, beliefs and patterns of behaviour which are disempowering
- develop new empowering beliefs and ways of behaving in the world
- understand and be aware of your thought processes, emotions, and behaviours
- stay focused on your purpose, goals and what is important to you
- be authentic and true to yourself and others about your values, beliefs and who you are
- raise your spiritual vibration to enhance your connection and work with Spirit

WHEN & WHERE?

Many people, if not most, centre their energy before they ground and again after any spiritual work. Alternatively, you can centre your energy in any given moment when you feel the need.

HOW?

You can centre yourself and bring all your energy back into the centre of your body in various ways. Some of the most popular ways in which you can do this are outlined below. It is important that you find which method or combination of methods work best for you.

BREATHE

Many of you are likely to centre yourselves regularly without being conscious that is what you are doing. The quickest and most convenient way to centre yourself is to take a deep breath in which brings your focus back to the present moment and helps you to become consciously aware of your thoughts, feelings and actions. Focusing on your breath is also a very   simple way to clear your mind of any excess chatter by bringing yourself back to a space where you feel peaceful and calm. You can do this by simply taking several slow deep breaths through your nose and out through your mouth, bringing your attention to your breathing for a few moments, or until you feel relaxed. So, anytime that your thoughts or energy seems scattered you can quieten and centre them by taking a few deep breaths.

JOURNALING

The most important part of becoming centered is to become fully aware of who you are, that is to get in touch with your authentic self. Journaling is an extremely powerful way to help you become centered and more consciously aware your own thoughts, memories, feelings, sensations, actions and environment. By writing down your daily experiences, thoughts and feelings you are learning more about who you are by allowing yourself the space to be completely open and honest and to gain clarity about what is working and what is not working for you, so that you can make positive choices which help you to step forward. Journaling also allows you to take time out to consciously reflect on events and circumstances within your life so that you can then start looking for the learning in them and see them from a different, higher, perspective. You may also begin to uncover layers of beliefs and patterns of behaviour which do not serve you and block your path so that you can then begin taking steps to let go of these beliefs and patterns and find your authentic self. One way in which you can begin this process is by:

1. Writing down a list of words that describes who you want to be, who you believe you can be

2. Write down another list of words that describe who you are today

3. Look at these two lists and compare how many words are the same or different on each

4. Reflect on and consider what changes you might be able to make in order to more fully align yourself with who you want to be

By journaling, you will also be more fully connected to your intuition and Spirit, therefore, increasing your spiritual vibration. This helps you to be more aware of the guidance you are receiving within your everyday life. When you are journaling, you can also ask for assistance and guidance with specific issues when required and gain knowledge about how your spiritual gifts work by connecting with yourself rather than allowing others to tell you how to work.

FOOD & EXERCISE

In order to become more centered, it is important that you consciously taking care of your physical body and that you are aware of the foods you are putting into it. It is extremely important to consider the effect that the food you are putting into your body has on your energy, not just in the short term but in the long term as well. Also, to maintain a healthy physical body with light and vibrant energy, it is important that you undertake some form of exercise such as a brisk walk, light jog or other cardiovascular activity at least 2-4 times per week. Yoga or martial arts can also help you shift energy around your body without losing balance physically and spiritually, therefore, keeping you very centered in your body. By making conscious decisions regarding your food and exercise habits within each moment, you will be able to create new patterns of behaviour which will enable your energy to flow freely and reduce the likelihood of dis-ease.

WALK A LABYRINTH

A labyrinth is a type of mandala which has been around for over 4000 years and is an integral part of many cultures including Native American, Greek, Celtic and Mayan. They are found in many sizes and shapes, and are created from sand, cornmeal, flour, painted, string, and can be built from stones, rocks or turf or are formed naturally by mounds of earth, vegetation and other natural materials. A labyrinth is a truly sacred place which has one path which leads directly to the centre and back out again, with no dead ends, making them an ideal tool to help you centre. Walking a labyrinth is a personal experience which helps you to focus on the present moment, clear the mind, gain clarity, meditate and to consciously reflect on your life experiences and journey.

FACE & RELEASE FEARS

When you feel that your thoughts, emotions and actions are coming from a space of fear, it is important that you have the courage to consciously examine these fears, as they are what keep you stuck in old patterns of thinking, negative emotions and ways of behaving. By centering yourself and facing your fears the less likely they are to hold you back, the more the fear disappears and problems transform into opportunities. You can begin examining your fears by:

1. Educating yourself about what your fears are and why they exist
2. Understand and become conscious of how these fears have played out in your life
3. Prepare yourself for how you will step up and take charge by facing your fears if they come up again
4. Release and let go of any irrational fears and replace them with more rational thoughts, emotions and behaviours which help you to move forward.

If you see, hear or sense Spirits and you become fearful, this could be stopping you from moving forward with your spiritual journey. To conquer your fear, you must have the courage to educate, inform and prepare yourself so that you can take charge of how and when you receive information. You can begin to do this by setting up boundaries with Spirit around how you wish to work and when. Further details about creating boundaries are included in chapter 6 on Spiritual Protection. This will help you to develop trust (the opposite of fear) and be able to consciously talk to your Spirit Guides about your boundaries so that information comes to you at a pace that you feel more comfortable. Remember, that fear attracts more things to be fearful of, which can include Spirits who have passed over who were fearful while they were on this Earth, so it is important that you have the courage to take charge as the communication with Spirit is a two-way process and you are in control.

PEOPLE

People who are not centered have a lower level of consciousness, are those focused on their external needs, living in the past, fearful (particularly about the future), negative in their words, thoughts and emotions and generally indifferent about life. If you are continually associating with people at this energetic vibration, then this will also result in your vibration being lowered. Therefore, in order to remain centered, it is important for you to surround yourself with people who have an internal focus, are present and consciously aware. This will then help you to remain centered, raise your consciousness and spiritual vibration. You can also spend time with those who are at a higher spiritual vibration so that you can learn from their experiences, gain ideas and further awareness about how to remain centered and conscious in the present.

SPEAK YOUR TRUTH

You can begin to live more consciously and become more centered by having the courage to speak your truth. To begin speaking your truth openly and honestly, it is important to look at which area(s) of your life (relationship, work, family etc) where your thoughts, words and actions do not match. Be honest with yourself and others about what you think and feel even if they disagree with you. Consider whether there are reasons why you might not be fully expressing your truth. For example ask yourself the following questions:

1. Is there anything that you are avoiding by not speaking your truth?
2. Are you fearful of how others might respond to you if you say what you think and feel?
3. Is there a particular outcome that you are attempting to achieve by speaking your truth?
4. Are you benefiting from not saying how you feel and what you think?
5. Is there a cost involved in you not speaking up?

When you have the courage to speak your truth you are also able to say 'no' to people when it does feel right for you without feeling guilty that you may have hurt their feelings. If you do things for others because you feel you 'should', you are behaving in ways that meet other people's expectations. This can leave you feeling angry, frustrated and annoyed because you have   spent time and energy doing the right thing by other people and not the right thing by yourself. It is important to be conscious of when you use the word 'should', other people's or societies expectations, and choose   to use 'will', 'choose' or 'must' instead. Remember, you have the right to say 'no' without feeling guilty. When speaking your truth it is important to:

1. Clearly identify what it is that you want (do not focus on what you don't want)
2. Directly and clearly communicate the behaviour or action you would like to see happen to the person or people involved
3. Own your thoughts and feelings by using personalised 'I' statements such as "I disagree with you" (instead of 'You're wrong') or "I'd like you to arrive in time in the future"(instead of 'You should be on time, you know')
4. Practice, practice, practice speaking your truth every day so that you become more confident and comfortable
5. Respect the other person's feelings as they are more likely to hear you when you speak from the truth in your heart

So, take a deep breath, dig deep for the courage you have within you and be willing to speak your truth, trusting that the Universe fully supports you.

RELEASING & LETTING GO

If you begin to feel scattered or stressed as a result of having too many things happening at once and thoughts continuously running through your head, then you can try releasing and letting go to help you get back to your centre. One way in which you can release thoughts when the mind is doing too much talking, over-analysing, is to focus on and consciously acknowledge the thoughts which will in turn help you to 'get out of your head' and back to the present moment. When you feel like you are 'in your head' you are more than likely focusing too much on the past or the future, the 'what if's' or the 'will there be enough's'. If this happens, take a breath, clear your mind and refocus your thoughts on the present moment by selecting and deliberately directing your words and thoughts in a more peaceful way. Your mind often uses chatter to distract you or keep you calm in situations where you feel afraid, vulnerable, are in physical pain or to   protect itself, so you can also reflect on what is happening around you and how you are feeling so that you can learn to let them go.

You can also let go of emotions such as anger, grief, sadness, guilt etc by simply allowing yourself to fully experience and feel the emotion. It is also important not to judge yourself for having feelings such as anger, frustration, depression, stress, worry etc because this will then mean that you need to release the thoughts or emotions which come up around judging yourself. Simply accept and let your feelings and thoughts to go with a gentle and persistent 'Its time to move on and let go', as this will help you to become more conscious and aware of what is not serving you in that moment. The release of these emotions may be experienced as a very deep cleansing breath, tears, movement of energy within and outside of your body or a general feeling of lightness in your physical body because you are no longer holding onto to unexpressed emotions. It is important to practice becoming aware of your thoughts and feelings in the moment, without judgment, so that you can make a conscious decision about whether the thought or feeling is worth keeping or letting go of.

Your beliefs are also energetically translated into feelings, thoughts and emotions, which in turn drive your behaviour and create your experiences. For example, if you believe that you are 'stupid' then your subconscious will take on that belief and you will limit yourself in terms of the educational opportunities you pursue. Likewise, if you have a belief that you have to 'work hard' to achieve your goals and desires then your subconscious will look for ways to make working towards your goals more difficult so that you work hard. If you believe you will always 'struggle financially' then this will also be your experience and if you do not believe you are attractive then you will also project that image to everyone around you.

Therefore, if you become aware of any beliefs which do not serve your highest good, then you can also begin to release and let go of these old beliefs and replace them with new ones. Remember, you are in control and get to make a conscious choice about what beliefs you continue to allow to drive your behaviour and create your experiences. So create a new reality today by releasing, letting go and shifting your beliefs.

GRATITUDE

To become more centered, it is important to shift your focus away from worrying about the future and appreciate the present, the 'now'. According to the Law of Attraction, by expressing your gratitude the more grateful you will become which attracts more things, situations, relationships, events and circumstances into your life to be grateful for. Expressing gratitude is a polite, daily thank you note to the Universe. To do this, you can express your gratitude to the Universe for all the great, wonderful things in your life (major and minor). Be thankful for minor things like the kindness of a stranger, the plumber turning up on time, the rock star park you got at the shops, your partner for picking the kids up after school, your housemate for taking out the rubbish, a hug from a friend, meeting a deadline, saying no to the fries with your meal. Express your gratitude for the major events as well, for example, your promotion, the new baby, big house, the engagement etc. By expressing your gratitude each day, you are placing your focus (thoughts and emotions) on positive experiences and away from the negative thoughts that block your ability to move forward on your journey. There are hundreds of ways to say thank you and express gratitude, none of which are wrong. The important thing is that you do say thank you and that you feel the gratitude deep in your heart.

VISUALISATION& MEDITATION

Visualisation involves using an internal focus to imagine surroundings or situations which represent a need or desire rather than on an external object. 'Centering' is often associated with meditation and simply means taking the time to be in the moment, to focus and be at peace. It is also a great way to practice focusing your attention within rather than on the external world or on the past or future. Meditation is simple to learn, as it just requires you to sit quietly, breathe deeply and tune out any distracting thoughts that pop into your mind. Being able to tune out and simply focus on your breath does take practice, so please don't give up if you don't master it the first time. To support you in staying centered, listen to my Sacred Self Meditation which helps you to connect to your inner self, become more present in the moment as well as more aware of your inner wisdom and intuition.

It is necessary to centre yourself in order to have the focus necessary to meditate, visualise, or do magic or healing. Spiritual energy and all of the joys of life feel good and yet you

66

have to become aware of how you may be blocking yourself and lowering your energy. You can learn to and consciously choose to open yourself up to the beautiful loving Universal energy always available to you and when you do, your life will change for the better and move forward.

CHAPTER 3. SPIRITUAL GROUNDING

Grounding is the first technique anyone undertaking a spiritual journey needs to master as this is the foundation upon which everything else is built. It is very simple and very powerful. Many of you may have heard of grounding or have practiced or used this technique in some form or another, whether consciously or unconsciously. So, let's start with an explanation about what people mean when they talk about "grounding".

WHAT?

Grounding is the act of consciously connecting the human energy field into this physical reality and that of the Earth (Mother Earth - Gaia). When you ground your energy you are consciously being here in the present moment, being aware of yourself physically, your surroundings, and your connection to the earth, while also striving to be more spiritual.

WHY?

Grounding creates a strong connection between your physical body and Mother Earth so that you are more aware of the sensations and energy flowing in your own body as well as what is happening in world around you. It helps you to become more fully present and conscious in your life, so that you can respond to the world and situations around you immediately and appropriately. The act of grounding helps you to stay in the present moment, let go of the past and trust that the future will be even better. Grounding also allows you to be able to release or let go of unwanted or excess energy whether your own or energy you may have picked up/taken on from external sources (person or object) so that it can be transformed into positive healing energy. Being grounded may help you to:

- Balance physical and emotional state
- Accept and deal with life in a secure and rational manner
- Be aware of your path
- Be conscious of your energy and where it is directed
- Release energy more easier
- Move through uncomfortable times more quickly
- Create a bridge between you and Spirit
- Connect with your higher self through intuition and meditation
- Trust Spirit and your intuition
- Stand in your power and strength and speak your truth
- Reduce stress and anxiety
- Lower blood pressure

When you come into your body more fully, you are going to start to become aware of what your body is actually feeling. The minute you ground, you align with the body and begin to tune in to what's actually going on. So, you may notice that you become aware of aches or pains in your body that were not there moments before. This helps you to begin to take steps to release and heal whatever is causing the problem. The body has much wisdom to teach you if you listen to what it is telling you. If you ignore the body, it will get louder and louder in an effort to get your attention. But you don't have to wait, you can begin the process of grounding before you are 'forced 'to by circumstances.

WHEN & WHERE?

Grounding is a skill you can use consistently, anywhere and anytime, in your day to day life. However, it is at the times when you are 'ungrounded' that you most need to use this technique. Generally, when someone says to you that you are 'ungrounded' or 'not well grounded' they mean that your energetic field is out of balance in a way that keeps you from connecting fully with your inner source of strength and power. If you are not grounded, then you are likely to experience some of the following physical sensations:

- Unaware of physical environment
- Focusing on the past/future or reacting based on past experiences
- Arguing, uncontrolled emotions and extreme reactions
- Sensitivity to noise and light
- Headaches
- Dizziness
- Feeling 'Spaced Out' and unable to focus attention

- Nervy/on-edge
- Clumsiness
- Forgetfulness
- Daydreaming/falling asleep when meditating
- Electric shocks
- Muscle spasms, trembling, excessive perspiration
- Incomplete ideas or ideas not acted on
- Feeling sick/nauseous
- Flickering eyes
- Inability to express thoughts/emotions
- Weight gain

Note: Many of these symptoms can also be linked to other physical conditions or illnesses, if in doubt always check with your GP. Light and energy work is complementary to general medicine and should not be viewed as a substitute.

When you start to feel any of the above sensations of being 'ungrounded', it is important that you get your energy grounded so that you start to feel calm, in control and have more clarity about what is going on around you. Because grounding involves connecting your energy with Mother Earth, the best place to ground your energy is outside in nature. However, you can ground your energy virtually anywhere. While working, studying, playing, eating, making love, shopping, driving, etc., as well as during ritual, or while meditating. This will help you to become more consciously present in your physical body and increase your capacity to experience wonderful things throughout your everyday life.

As you begin developing your intuition and working with Spirit, where possible you should try to make reconnecting to Mother Earth and   grounding your energy a part of your daily routine. You also need to ensure that you ground your energy before you undertake any work with Spirit including readings, healings, magic or spell-casting, or rituals as it increases your spiritual vibration and helps you to open to and be a clear channel for divine energies. By grounding your energy first, you become less receptive to taking on negative or lower energies and minimize the risk of harm to yourself and those you are working with.

How?

There are many different grounding techniques you can use which are easy to work with. Most grounding methods work best if you have both your feet firmly placed on the ground or floor. You may need to try a few different methods or adapt them to suit your own needs and what you feel comfortable with. While it is impossible to cover all of the techniques available, a few different methods are provided below so that you can experiment and see which one(s) work best for you.

FOOD & WATER

Grounding foods bring your energy down from your head to your stomach, so eating healthy and well balanced foods is important. Foods associated with the root (base) chakra such as potatoes, radishes, onions, turnips, peanuts, carrots, beets, garlic, and so on are extremely good for helping you ground your energy. Dehydration is also one of the biggest energetic weaknesses that most people have, so it is important to make sure you drink plenty of water to help your energy flow easily throughout your body and to bring yourself back to Earth.

PHYSICAL EXERCISE

Any exercise which uses and develops physical strength is good for grounding as it will help to ease you out of your head (thoughts) and recreate a healthy balance between your body and mind. Depending on what you feel comfortable with any of the following forms of physical exercise might be useful:

- Walking, especially barefoot in nature (quickest method)
- Yoga, tai chi etc.
- Intense aerobic exercise
- Team sport
- Sex
- Housework, laundry, shopping (acts as a 'moving meditation')

GARDENING

Gardening is also an effective way to ground your energy as it allows you to have hands on involvement with Mother Earth. The garden can also help you to learn about nature, develop patience and creativity, help still the mind from some of your cares and worries, relax, unwind, smile, and enjoy the world around you.

ANIMALS

Animals, in their innocence, provide a clear and clean mirror for us to see ourselves and as such are very powerful to help in grounding your energy. If you have a dog take it for a walk or sit and pet your cat until you feel like you are grounded.

MUSIC/SINGING

Music with deep notes which resonate with the root (base) chakra, specifically drumming, helps you to maintain your connection to the Earth by staying grounded. Likewise, singing the deepest note you can and feeling it vibrate deep in your belly and pelvis then extending deep into the earth also helps you to ground.

CRYSTALS

Crystals carry Earthing energy because they grew and developed in the Earth. Carrying, wearing or placing crystals on your body or placing them around your home or office can help to ground your energy. The best crystals for grounding energy are generally dark or earthy in colour. Some of the most popular crystals to help you ground your energy include:

- Hematite
- Red jasper (or any other jasper)
- Petrified Wood

- Tigers eye
- Pyrite or Copper

Any of the above crystals can be carried in pouches or worn as jewellery throughout the day or while meditating to help ground your energy. You can also place them between your feet while watching TV or while you are in the office working.

AFFIRMATIONS

Every thought you have, every word you say, is an order you put out into the Universe which creates and attracts to you various experiences within your life. Affirmations help you to become more conscious of the thoughts and words you are sending out and allow you to focus on the experiences you want to attract. You can use any of the following affirmations when you first wake up, throughout the day, before you go to bed or any other time you feel the need to ground your energy:

- I stay focused on the present and respond to situations peacefully
- I release all anxiety, fear and worry, knowing all is well
- I remain present in each moment
- I am grounded, focused and safe
- I trust that all is unfolding exactly as it is meant to
- I am strong and speak my truth from a place of love
- I trust my intuition and allow Spirit to guide me

Visualisation & Meditation

You can use visualisations by drawing the focus to the internal world and imagine surroundings or situations which represent the need or desire to ground rather than placing the focus on an external object. Meditation is also a great way to quiet and calm the mind, help to rest and rejuvenate the body, mind and spirit through a process of deep relaxation. Listen to my   Grounding with the Earth Meditation to help you create a solid foundation in the physical world upon which you can plant your feet so you are able to be more present in your daily life, to be more consciously aware and in the moment as well as anchoring your energy bodies into the physical world while striving to be more spiritual.

Some people are able to feel that they are grounded and connected to Mother Earth by feeling a slight buzzing, warmth or tingling under the sole of each foot. However, it may take some time to become aware of these feelings as it takes training and lots of practice. If you are unable to feel these sensations then you can confirm whether or not you are grounded by balancing on one leg. If you are properly grounded, you will find it easy to do, and you should be able to move the other leg around in the air without losing your balance. With lots of practice and regular grounding you will find that you can ground yourself within seconds just by thinking of grounding or by turning your attention to the soles of your feet. Remember, you might need to try a few different techniques until you find what feels right for you.

CHAPTER 4. BALANCING

Life is often like walking a tightrope, with your success or failure depending on how well you are able to remain balanced with all aspects of your life. While there are many facets of life which call for balance, when you hear people speak about 'balance' they are saying that it is important that you try to ensure you are stable mentally, physically, emotionally and spiritually, in other words, in your inner and external worlds.

MASCULINE & FEMININE

We all have both masculine and feminine aspects within us regardless of gender, which makes us whole and complete. It is important to be able to balance, integrate and fully express both your masculine and feminine energy. Masculine energy is directed, focused, rigorous, logical and action orientated. It is portrayed as strength, courage, wisdom, power, dominance, leadership, charisma, presence, independence, assertiveness and self confidence when fully expressed. When your thoughts are focused on the material world you are in your masculine energy and seeking protection, safety and security. You would also be expressing masculine energy if you see your own rights as being more valid or important than the rights of others. The stronger the masculine energy, the greater your sex-drive and the more aggressive you are said to be sexually.

Below is a list of qualities you might display if your masculine energy is unbalanced:

- More easily become angry and aggressive
- Feel unjustly treated by others
- Unrealistically high opinion of your own rights compared to those of others
- Greed and selfishness, wanting more than your fair share or obtaining things at others expense
- Pushy, take unfair advantage of and exploit other people

On the other hand, feminine energy is intuitive, receptive, passive and sometimes vague. It is expressed through emotions, subtle communication, intuition, relationships, radiance, love, spontaneity as well as your ability to surrender and go with the flow. When your energy is introspective, nurturing, warm and kind, you have a sense of well-being and are in your feminine energy. You would also be expressing feminine energy if you think of other people's rights as being more valid and important than your own. The stronger the feminine energy the more giving you are likely to be sexually and the more enjoyable you will find your sexual experiences. Below is a list of qualities you might display if your feminine energy is unbalanced:

- More easily become fearful and defensive
- Feel you are treating others unjustly

- Unrealistic low opinion of your own rights as compared to those of others
- Allow others to take advantage of you and become a doormat for people
- Low level of self-confidence and become angry with yourself easily because you not living up to your potential

However, if your masculine and feminine energies are out of balance, you may be a woman who is displaying mostly masculine qualities and vice-versa. If you are unbalanced on the feminine side you are likely to give up your rights in order to allow someone else to acquire more than they are entitled to, sometimes resulting in you being taken advantage of.

When masculine and feminine energy are in balance, they compliment each other and your mind and heart are in alignment. This will enable you to express yourself openly and honestly, while respecting and having compassion for others and to directly align with your core values. It also allows you to connect with what you are passionate about as well as align with your life purpose, that is, what inspires and nourishes your soul. Therefore, balancing your masculine/feminine energy is not only important in your daily life but also in your work with Spirit.

LIGHT (POSITIVE) & DARK (NEGATIVE)

Most of you will have the perception that light is good and darkness is evil because this is what you have been conditioned to believe. You may believe that light allows you to see things and understand what is going on, it provides warmth and is a giver of life. However, when you stand in the darkness, you feel afraid because you can't see and don't know what is coming at you. However, all things exist in balance, therefore, light and dark energy are related and are in fact mirrors of one another. It has been suggested that darkness is simply light standing still, ready to become light. Therefore, darkness is the source of light. When you walk a spiritual path, it is necessary to seek the light within the darkness and to also recognise the darkness within the light. It is important to journey into the darkness, also known as the shadow side, so that you are able to bring it into conscious awareness and transform it into light. For example, most alcoholics or drug addicts tend to be running from something that they do not want to face, people suffering from depression often fear their own anger, and those who are incredibly anxious often fear the unknown. Therefore, it is important to look for the balance between light and dark so that you are able to see things more clearly and have a greater understanding of what is happening.

GIVING & RECEIVING

The second area within your life and in your work with Spirit, where it is important to find balance, is giving and receiving. Giving does not exist without someone receiving and you cannot receive without someone giving, so one requires the other in order for either to happen. When you practice giving, you are active, purposeful, affirming, directed and your energy is flowing outward to others. When you are giving you are willing to give, whether possessions, time, knowledge, resources or energy to others, rather than trying to hang on to what you have received for yourself. However, it is important to be conscious of the reasons why you are giving to ensure that you are not creating negative energy around you which can result in negative experiences. The following are some reasons why you may give which can create negative energy:

- Feel like you have to or are 'expected' to
- Feel worthy and valued
- Not feel guilty
- Wanting something emotionally or physically in return
- 'Look good' and abundant
- Help yourself feel better
- Fulfill a need or want for you or for someone else

When you give for any of the above reasons, you attach negative emotions and energy such as ego, control, resentment, anger, hurt and need to act which limit and separate you from the joy and flow of giving and receiving. In other words, it stops the flow of attracting positive results and abundance from the act of both giving and receiving. Therefore, it is important to reflect and be consciously aware of your reasons for giving and where necessary, shift any negative emotions and beliefs surrounding this and take positive steps to make changes in this area.

When you practice receiving, you are more passive, accepting, non- directed and even surrender which is an inward flow of energy. In order to receive you must be able to give, as well as be open to receiving and taking the opportunities, knowledge and abundance that comes your way, no matter how small, which serves the highest good of all. It is just as important to examine and become consciously aware how you receive for yourself as how you give, because you can also create negative energy around receiving.

Giving and receiving happens to you all, every day of your life, whether you are conscious of it or not. As you grow spiritually, one of the areas you will be asked to develop and experience is the ability to balance giving and receiving. When you give and receive in balance, or create a fair exchange, you will find positive energy comes into your life which is then shared and extended to others around you and within the world. When you are consciously aware of how, what, where, when and why you give and receive within the world, you have the ability to prevent negative experiences, emotions and situations which lead to resentment, disappointment, feeling unfulfilled, guilt, anger, hurt and sadness not only for you but for others as well.

PHYSICAL & SPIRITUAL

If you carry out spiritual, energetic, healing and magical work, it is also essential that you work to balance your energies by living in the physical world and don't live too much in the spiritual. There are three main areas which need to be considered and balanced when looking at the physical and spiritual world, your practice, the intent behind your practice and the space from which you live your life and undertake your work.

Firstly, the foundation of any spiritual development, involves participating in formal practice such as meditation, ritual or communication with Spirit in order to bring together and transform energies, exercise your spirit and help you to explore your inner self at a deeper level. In combination with your formal practice, it is equally important to continuously practice awareness of the physical world around you as well as any physical sensations in your body. By being physically present in the world you will also develop your spiritual gifts and can begin asking for help from Spirit as you go about your everyday life. While continuous practice may not be as deep as when you sit in formal practice, if it is sustained and frequent throughout the day, you will find that you are deeply centered and balanced by the end of the day. It is also extremely important to find a balance between your formal and continuous practice because you can't spend your entire day in meditation or you will not experience this beautiful world we live in.

Secondly, when you undertake spiritual work, it is important to be aware of your intentions for doing so and to make sure you maintain a healthy balance between your personal physical needs and being of service to Spirit. If you place too much focus on yourself, you risk becoming self- absorbed, coming from ego and losing sight of the greater purpose for your work. However, if you focus solely on being of service to others, you risk losing yourself, losing energy and the peace of mind you need in order to effectively be of service to Spirit. If you focus exclusively on Spirit, then you may risk losing your focus on this beautiful world you live in, losing your ability to relate well to others and the environment. Therefore, it is extremely important that you create a balance between self-directed desires, serving others and/or Spirit so that a sense of completeness and integrity may result.

The third area looks at the space, whether the body, heart, mind or spirit, that you operate from within both your everyday life and when doing spiritual work. When you operate from your physical body you are able to move, act and maintain life within the material world. Operating from your heart enables you to explore and experience the full range of emotions within your inside and outside world. If you operate from the mind, you have the ability to recognise, think, visualise, plan, imagine, daydream, remember and understand. Your spirit is typically hidden and has the power to unify your body, heart and mind through daily practices which aim to reconnect you with your true essence, your soul. Most people tend to be unbalanced by living permanently in their thoughts, or feelings or in their physical abilities and desires. Therefore, as you start your spiritual development, it is important to work on finding a balance between the body, mind and emotions and to go within to reconnect with your spirit.

ENERGY BODIES & CHAKRA'S

Each of your chakra's, the energy centres through which spiritual/universal energy flows in to and out of your aura, 'spin' and radiate their own unique frequency which indicates if they are 'open' (operating normally), blocked, 'not open' enough (under- active) or 'too open' (over-active). When your energy bodies and chakra's are balanced, the energy flows freely through each chakra, you feel energetic, creative and at peace as well as experience health, vitality and wellbeing. Below is a list of what you feel and experience when each individual chakra is open and balanced:

- **Base:** Centered, grounded, ability to plan, practical, disciplined, strive for excellence, vitality, hope, joy, harmony, wholeness, manifest, abundant, prosperous, stable, safe and secure

- **Sacral:** Freedom. mercy, forgiveness, justice, friendly, graceful, outgoing, loves to laugh, ability to experience pleasure and intimacy, passionate, ability to change and transform, intuition, prophecy, magic, creative, enthusiastic for life, nurtures self and others

- **Solar Plexus:** Confident, strong self-esteem, personal power, respects boundaries, responsible, reliable, selfless service, desire, expressive, spontaneous, playful, sense of humour, meets challenges, peaceful, balanced, warm

- **Heart:** Unconditional love, compassion, beauty, willing to help, empathic, appreciation, warm, sincere, happy, friendly, outgoing, peaceful, balanced, charitable, generous

- **Throat:** Creative, imaginative, expressive, present, speaks truth, listens in truth, power, will, trust, faith, protection, purposeful, courageous, openly shares knowledge

- **Third Eye:** Guidance, intuition, clairvoyance, vision, clarity, focus, truth, healing, imagination, visualisation, manifestation, integrate information from different levels, access past lives, astral travel

- **Crown:** Connection to Spirit, wisdom, self-knowledge, understanding, open-minded, aware, consciousness, ability to perceive, analyse and assimilate information, able to see patterns of beliefs, emotions and behaviours

When one or more of your chakras are blocked and the flow is inhibited, this can cause fatigue, illness, disease and mental and emotional imbalances. Some of the signs that particular energy centres are blocked include:

- **Base:** Inability to ground, overeating, obesity, denial, disconnected, alienated, discouraged, hopeless, chaotic, mood swings, inability to manifest, lack of energy, fear of safety and survival. poor circulation, varicose veins, lower back pain, swollen hands and legs, fluid retention, dry skin and hair, constipation, pale blotchy skin, belching, gas, diarrhea, headaches

- **Sacral:** Depressed, mood swings, physical problems with kidneys, spleen, frequent painful urination, lower back pain, swollen hands and feet, puffed, bloated, menstruation difficulties, pain in legs or groin

- **Solar Plexus:** Anxiety, stress, worry, easy to become angry or agitated, problems with the stomach, liver, gall bladder, spine, puffed, bloated, belching, gas, diarrhea/constipation, sugar or salt cravings, restless sleep, middle back pain, thirsty all the time

- **Heart:** chest pain, lungs, pasty complexation, upper back tension, blood pressure and circulation problems, cold sweats, tight muscles, immune deficiency, sadness, grief, depression, guilt, disappointment, hurt, fear, anger

- **Throat:** Communication problems, throat issues, respiratory diseases, lung problems, colds, tickle or phlegm in throat, coughing, stress, hyperactivity, allergies, fatigue, binge eating or drinking, dental disorders, low self-esteem
- **Third Eye:** Fear of intuitive insights, imagination, dreams, sinus/nose congestion, insomnia, difficulty concentrating and making decisions, headaches, depression, hormonal difficulties, poor vision, problems with hypothalamus, autonomic nervous system, anxiety
- **Crown:** Migraines, schizophrenia, tired, poor coordination, short term memory, hallucination, ringing in the ears, problems with upper brain, right eye

Some of the common signs that your chakras are 'not open' (under- active) and out of balance include:

- **Base:** Weak, tired, lack of stamina, sluggish, lazy, overly cautious, afraid of change, sexually manipulative, possessive, needs approval, lacks confidence, fearful, anxious, restless, poor boundaries, no trust in life, unable to meet goals, poor focus, undisciplined, chronic disorganisation, financial difficulty
- **Sacral:** Unemotional, standoffish, distrust, poor social skills, introverted, unable to express emotions, denies

pleasure, lacks passion and excitement, excessive boundaries, fear of change, fear of sex

- **Solar Plexus:** Passive, indecisive, timid, easily manipulated, poor discipline and willpower, inability to learn, seeking recognition, depressed, feel isolated, unreliable, lacking confidence, fear, anxiety
- **Heart:** Hatred, dislike, selfishness, possessive, moody, anti-social, withdrawn, melodramatic, paranoid, indecisive, afraid of intimacy, lonely, isolated, feels rejected, lack of empathy and compassion, feeling unloved, self-pity, negligence, needs reassurance of worth
- **Throat:** Fear of speaking, not trusting intuition, difficulty putting feelings into words, shy, quiet, withdrawn, cowardice, doubt, slow to respond, resistant to change, stubborn
- **Third Eye:** Inflexible, lack of imagination, vision and clarity, difficulty seeing future, easily lose head under stress, worries, fearful, unassertive, undisciplined, afraid of success, self-doubt
- **Crown:** Fear of or cynical of spirituality, feels separated from abundance and wholeness, little joy, learning difficulties, uncertainty, lack of purpose, frustration, unrealised power, needs sympathy

Common indications that your chakras are 'too open' (over-active) and out of balance include:

- **Base:** Hyperactive, aggressive, domineering, sexually-oppressive, egotistic, reckless, impulsive, greedy, materialistic, hoarding, fear of change, addiction to safety and security, rigid boundaries
- **Sacral:** Addiction to pleasure, sexual addiction, overindulgent, overly sensitive, selfish, arrogant, intolerant, unforgiving, lack of tact, disregard for others, power hungry, overly proud, emotionally explosive, obsessive, poor boundaries
- **Solar Plexus:** Judgemental, righteous, stubborn, arrogant, overly aggressive, domineering, controlling, manipulative, cold emotionally and physically, power hungry, deceptive, temper tantrums, anger, victim mentality, blames others, competitive, ambitious, workaholic, perfectionist
- **Heart:** Co-dependence, jealousy, clinging, critical, judgemental, demanding, over-sacrificing, stingy, angry, overconfident
- **Throat:** Talking too much, domineering, control, arrogant, self-righteous, gossip, inability to listen, forceful, anger, hospitality, resentment, course and deliberate language
- **Third Eye:** Difficulty concentrating, obsessed, delusions, hallucinations, nightmares, fearful, belittles others, egotistic, manipulative
- **Crown:** Overly intellectual, confused, spiritual addiction, vanity, disassociation from the body,

misunderstood, shame, negative image of self, ego-centered, narrow-minded, ignorant

If these imbalances persist over time, they may eventually affect your energy to the point of developing physical ailments or even dis-ease, so it is important to balance your energy in order to remain physically healthy. It is also important to help keep you calm amidst the busy-ness of everyday life, be more focused and pleasant to others and not allow your inner light to be overshadowed by stressful circumstances or negative thoughts and emotions. Remember, feelings of being unclear, unfocused, stress and off balance, can all be signs that one (or more) of your chakra's is blocked and the energy is not flowing harmoniously through them, or it is wide open, resulting in imbalances in your physical body, thoughts, emotions and behaviour.

WHEN & WHERE?

Some people suggest balancing to help you with whatever visualisation you wish to do to ground. Others suggest grounding first. The bottom line is that if you are hopelessly ungrounded, you probably won't be able to balance too well. So it is suggested that you use one of the more physical techniques to get grounded and then balance. You can balance yourself anywhere, anytime in just a few minutes. Whether this is when you are working and your thoughts seem to get scattered or while you're visiting family eating, shopping, driving, while meditating etc. Depending on your lifestyle and how blocked or open you are, you may need to balance your energies several times a day, once a week, or twice a month. Each person is different and handles life in different ways, so it's really up to you how often you feel you need to do this.

How?

There are many different ways to balance your energies, but every one of us is different, and some of you will have more success with one technique than another. If you try some of these techniques and they don't seem to work for you, try adjusting or combining several methods until you find something that works for you.

GRATITUDE

A large part of finding a balance between giving and receiving starts with being grateful for and consciously aware of your blessings. One of the fastest ways to improve/re-balance your energy when your thoughts, emotions and actions have been negative, is to start thinking about things for which you are grateful. By being grateful you will open your mind to new possibilities and connections and view challenges or issues as opportunities to learn, grow and improve. When counting your blessings, it is also important to be grateful for the big things, like your family and friends who love, support and help you as well as the little things, like the door which was opened for you or the coffee you had made this morning. An 'attitude of gratitude' will not only help you to be able to attract more things to be grateful for, but will help you feel happier and more optimistic. You can adopt an 'attitude of gratitude' by simply mentally or on a piece of paper, making a list of at least five things you have to be grateful for each night before you go to bed or first thing in the morning. If there is a person you can thank or show your appreciation to, then make a phone call or send them an email letting them know how grateful you are.

MUSIC/SOUND

Music has a fantastic way of making people feel different, more relaxed and less stressed, particularly certain styles of music. Our Chakras also resonate to sound, and when music/sound in different pitches is played, our bodies absorb the musical energies and help bring you back to balance, to stabilise your energy system, which in turn helps to calm your body down, bring it into a more relaxed and less stressful state. Next time you listen to a piece of music, try and feel the music and let it work its wonders on your body, play an instrument in a key associated with a Chakra within the region you feel might be in need of some help:

- Crown - "B"
- Third Eye - "A" and "Bb"
- Throat - "G" and "G#"
- Heart - "F" and "F#"
- Solar Plexus - "E" and "Eb"
- Sacral - "D" and "C#"

- Base - "C"

YOGA

Yoga is an ancient practice that increases the flow of energy in your life. In other words, yoga helps create a sense of union with and balances the body, mind, and spirit. A regular practice of yoga will help you to find a balance between the body, heart, mind or spirit. The warrior yoga poses can help if you tend to be nurturing, agreeable and play the 'nice' role by meeting everyone else's needs but your own and need to bring in more masculine energy to get you back into balance. Alternatively, you can try a more relaxing form of yoga if you need to slow down and bring in more feminine energy.

PEOPLE

It is extremely important to find a balance between spending time with those who raise your consciousness and with those you can help. Learn from those who are a little more conscious, and help those who are a little less conscious than you. In this manner you serve the highest good of all, expanding consciousness everywhere. It is also important in order to balance your masculine and feminine energies to spend time with healthy role models. These role models can be people within your life, or if you can't find anyone appropriate, imagine the qualities of a balanced woman and a balanced man.

SUNLIGHT

Sunlight is our main source of light, heat and energy. Light consists of the seven colour energies: red, orange, yellow, green, blue, indigo and violet which are contained in a rainbow, drop of rain or dew and even in a snowflake. Many body functions are stimulated or slowed down by light and the different colours of light and thus affect your chakra system. Therefore, spending time out in sunlight will help you to balance your masculine and feminine energy, energy bodies as well as your aura.

COLOUR

Colour is all around us from the time we were born and it affects our everyday life in many ways. By becoming aware of the power of colour and its effects on your energies, you can learn how to make positive changes in specific areas of your life, use if for healing and to bring balance and harmony within the mind and body. Depending what colour you choose, the invisible vibration of colour can relax or stimulate. You can use colour to help balance your energy by wearing it, placing it in your environment and/or visualising it glowing brightly around the appropriate charka.

HERBS & INCENSE

For centuries our ancestors ate, drank, burned and otherwise used herbs (plant or plant part) for healing and magic to ward off evil, attract prosperity, protect children and women in labour, and to heal illnesses. The burning of herbs or incense is a sacred practice and works on the physical, emotional, mental, spiritual and magical levels. Sometimes branches of herbs are placed directly into an open fire but they are most often a piece of charcoal placed in a container (eg. cauldron or abalone shell) and the herbs are sprinkled on the hot coals. The main idea is to release the herbs energy and fragrance near to the certain chakra you want to stimulate and help increase the general flow of energy and to balance your energies. The following herbs can be linked to each of the seven chakras:

- **Base:** Basil, Patchouli, Tea Tree
- **Sacral:** Orange, Jasmine, Ylang-Ylang
- **Solar Plexus:** Lemon, Pine, Sage
- **Heart:** Chamomile, Lavender, Rose
- **Throat:** Eucalyptus, Lemongrass, Peppermint
- **Third Eye:** Geranium, Myrrh, Violet
- **Crown:** Bergamot, Frankincense, Sandalwood

While the energy and fragrance from the herbs pours through your chakra, you can visualise the smoke as different colours swirling in and around your body, filling you with radiant colour.

ESSENTIAL OILS

Sensory input can stimulate our emotional and physiological responses. In today's world we are constantly receiving sensory stimuli (eg. computers, fluorescent light, television, radio, hum of refrigerator, exhaust fumes etc). Of the five senses, our sense of smell is the most primitive and most closely associated with our emotions and how our body responds to them, so one of the best ways to relieve stresses and bring your body back into balance is through the use of essential oils. Essential oils are found in the seeds, roots, resins, flowers, trees, stems, bark and fruit of plants and provide many physical, emotional and spiritual benefits. Oils can become part of your daily routine through the use of a diffuser, spritzer/spray, anointing, massage and water/spa treatments to help you achieve a healthier, more balanced lifestyle. The following oils can be used with the chakras to help unblock or rebalance specific energy centres:

- **Base:** Ylang Ylang, Vetiver
- **Sacral:** Cedarwood, Tangerine, Pettigrain, Geranium
- **Solar Plexus:** Bergamot, Grapefruit, Rosemary, Lemongrass
- **Heart:** Eucalyptus, Peppermint, Rosewood
- **Throat:** Geranium, Lemon, Pepper, Sweet Birch
- **Third Eye:** Lavender, Magnolia, Ylang Ylang
- **Crown:** Frankincense, Garden

CRYSTALS

Crystals carry Earthing energy because they grew and developed in the Earth, therefore, carrying, wearing or placing crystals on your body can help to center and balance your energy. Crystals can be placed directly on blocked or over-active charkas to centre and balance the energy in that area, including:

- **Base:** Red Jasper, Garnet, Ruby, Obsidian, Smoky Quartz, Haematite
- **Sacral:** Tiger Eye, Carnelian, Orange Calcite
- **Solar Plexus:** Amber, Citrine, Rutile Quartz, Topaz
- **Heart:** Rose Quartz, Kunzite, Malachite, Pink Tourmaline, Rhodochrosite, Jade, Bloodstone, Green Aventurine
- **Throat:** Azurite, Aquamarine, Blue Lace Agate, Celestite, Sodalite
- **Third Eye:** Lapis lazuli, Sugilite, Fluorite
- **Crown:** Amethyst, Clear Quartz, Moonstone, Selenite

Any of the above crystals can be carried in pouches or worn as jewellery throughout the day or while meditating to help cleanse your energy. You can also place them on your computer screen or around your home and office.

Note: Remember to cleanse and charge your crystals before each use.

AFFIRMATIONS

Words and/or affirmations are very powerful tools in helping to balance our energies. You can do this by simply finding a quiet space to sit away from any distractions and breathe slowly and deeply. Then either choose a soothing word such as peace, love, or truth or a phrase (affirmation) and repeat it over and over in your mind. Any of the following affirmations can be used each day to balance your energy:

- I am balanced in every aspect of my life I balance work and play everyday
- My mind, body and spirit are well balanced and in harmony
- I am always deeply relaxed, centered and balanced in every way
- I am balanced in my head and heart
- My thoughts, goals, values and emotions are in balance
- Positive energy flows freely through my entire being
- I now live a balanced life, full of love, abundance, and miracles
- I acknowledge and rejoice in my spirituality
- I always receive and recognise the guidance I need
- I speak my truth gracefully, respectfully and confidently
- I am open to giving and receiving love, freely and effortlessly
- I forgive and release the pains of my past and am free to love in the present
- I stand in my power and accept responsibility for all areas of my life
- I listen to and learn from my emotions
- The Universe looks after my needs. I trust life
- I am well balanced because I am open to what the Universe has to offer

PENDULUM

You can use a pendulum to check whether your chakras are in balance by placing it over each chakra and asking the pendulum to show you the direction, size and speed of the energy in that area. You can also go through and ask each of the chakra questions that can be answered with a YES or NO. In the same manner you can determine if or what crystals or colours may be needed in order to bring them back into balance.

ENERGY HEALING

There are a variety of hands-on and hands-off energy healing techniques available which aim to restore harmony, energy and balance within the human energy system. Energy healing is a gentle, non-invasive technique where energy is directed through the healers hands to clear, energise and balance the human and environmental energy fields to promote physical, emotional, mental and spiritual health and well-being. A healer trained in manipulating the flow of energy can assist you get your chakras back into balance and functioning properly. There are many different types of Energy Healing including, but are not limited to, Reiki, Spiritual Healing, Energy-Focused Bodywork, Pranic Healing, Shamanic Healing and Theta Healing. These techniques may be extremely useful to compliment or in collaboration with conventional health care where various physical ailments including stress, depression, muscle tension, back and neck pain, emotional trauma, insomnia and illness or other medical concerns arise. Energetic healing provides a wide range of benefits such as increased energy, enhanced feeling of well-being, boosted self-esteem, stress relief and much more. Afterwards, there are also a variety of healthy actions you can take to help keep your chakra's open, allowing your energy to flow naturally.

Note: Energy healings are not meant to replace or substitute proper medical, psychological care or professional advice from other relevant practitioners. If you have a medical, health or psychological ailment you should see a medical or mental health professional for the appropriate professional care.

VISUALISATION & MEDITATION

Visualisations are a fantastic way to help bring your energies back into balance by allowing the focus to be moved from the external world to the inner world and imagining your and situations in peace. You can also go into meditation to help you relax, quieten and calm the mind as well as rejuvenate and rebalance the body, mind and spirit through. My Rainbow Bath Chakra Meditation will help you to clear, balance and open each of the seven centers of energy (Chakra's) physically and spiritually associated with various parts of our bodies so you are able to flow through life with ease, grace and joy.

CHAPTER 5. SPIRITUAL CLEANSING

When people speak of 'cleansing', they are not implying that you are 'dirty', they are suggesting that the energy body may be impure. As you move through this world and go about your daily life, especially when dealing with other people, over time you pick up bits of energy and emotions (psychic energy) from the people and things around you. These energies may be either positive (higher vibration) or negative (lower vibration) and get combined with and affect your own energy causing problems and having an effect on your daily life. Because these energies are not your own, it is important to cleanse yourself as required, of any lower or negative energies you may have absorbed throughout the day.

WHAT?

Psychic cleansing means that you cleanse the emotional, mental, and spiritual layers of your aura from all forms of impure intentions, negative energies, dark emotions, depressing thoughts, and other similar imbalances. As you begin working more closely with Spirit, whether as a healer, psychic, medium etc you will be highly sensitive to the different types of energy. If you come across people who may be feeling angry, frustrated, resentful, jealous or lonely, and so on, you could unconsciously pick up these emotions and carry them within your energy body. It is important to release these emotions as quickly as possible so that you reduce the impact they can have on your everyday life. Also, if your mind is cluttered with worries, doubts and fears, your energy body can be weakened and become more susceptible to picking up other people's fears and doubts which will keep you in your head and intensify the chat in your mind. No matter how conscious you are about the different energies around you, you may still pick up other peoples energy. Even walking through a crowded street you may, unconsciously, pick up other peoples stuff. Because you can pick up these energies unconsciously, it is important to consciously 'cleanse' your energy regularly by clearing, releasing and letting go of any unseen dirt, impurities and unwanted or excess energies. By getting rid of any of these negative energies from your aura you will clear away any grime and dirt you have collected and feel more peaceful as a result.

WHY?

It is important to cleanse your energy body so that you maintain clean, crisp energy around you and to ensure that you don't get clogged up with negative energies, whether they are your own or from other people. For example, if you have others energy around you, you can suddenly begin to feel anxious, lost, worried and ungrounded for no reasons at all. So, cleansing your energy field of negative energies can mean the difference between feeling blocked and depressed, and maybe even constipated and feeling refreshed, inspired, and full of ideas.

Also because you inadvertently share (pick and give) your energy with other people you come into contact with, it is also important to cleanse your own energy so that you do not go spreading around your negative energy to friends and family, or even strangers. For example, a bad working environment where there is an increase of negative energy can cause layer upon layer of difficulties including problems with co-workers, trouble with clients, even the break- down of electronic equipment like computers, printers, and copiers. So cleansing the environment is equally as important as cleansing yourself. There are enormous benefits within your everyday life to cleansing your energy including:

- Increased balance between the physical, mental, emotional and spiritual
- Reduces worry and negative thinking
- Helps calm and clear the mind
- Helps recharge your energy and increase spiritual, physical, or emotional healing
- Frees you from and prevents negativity
- Helps you radiate peace and joy within your life
- Increases your ability to clear out and let go of old energies and toxins to make way for the new (including ideas, thoughts, sensations, emotions, and so forth)
- Allows energy to freely flow through your body (including blood, oxygen, hormones)

WHEN & WHERE?

Once you learn how to cleanse your energy, you should make it a part of your routine each morning and before going to bed, just like washing your face or brushing your teeth. It is recommended that you cleanse your energy in the morning to prepare yourself for the day and again at night to cleanse yourself of what you may have picked up before you go to bed. Of course, you can use any of the techniques anywhere at any time during the day, as needed, especially if you are out in a shopping centre or other crowded places. It is recommended that you monitor your feelings and thoughts for negative changes, for example if you feel scattered, besieged, angry for no apparent reason these are all cues that you may need to cleanse your energy. You can also cleanse when you are about to start any sort of work, spiritual or otherwise, with other people to ensure that your energy is clear. However, the most important time to cleanse is after you have done any spiritual work, whether a healing or reading, in order to disconnect your energy from your client's.

HOW?

There are many different ways to cleanse unwanted energies from around and within your body which are easy to work with. Some of these are physical acts while others involve visualisations. You may need to try a few different methods or adapt them to suit your own needs and what you feel comfortable with. A few different exercises have been included below to help you start trying some of these techniques so that you can see which one(s) work best for you.

PLANTS

One of the simplest ways you can clear your energy field debris and toxins is by getting out into Mother Nature, as plants help to transmute lower energies into higher vibrations. To do this you can place a plant beside your bed as it will help with the release of heavier energy that you may have taken in throughout your day and sends it out into the Universe. If your work environment places you in a position where you may be open to taking on negative energies, whether from colleagues or clients, for example counselling, healing or massage, a plant in the space so that helps clear the environment. The larger and broader the leaves on the plants that you use, the more energy they are able to absorb and transform into positive.

BREATHE

You can cleanse your aura using nothing more elaborate than your breath. To do this you simply breathe in and then using the out breath you send any unwanted negative energies down into the Earth, cleansing you and grounding the energies at the same time. This technique is fast and subtle, so you can use it anywhere, anytime and no one will even know what you are doing.

WATER

Water, of course, is cleansing. Whether you sprinkle or spray water into your aura, take a bath or shower with hot water or even rain water, this will all help to cleanse you of any negative energies. You can also use saltwater, water infused with herbs or essential oils in a bath and sit back and feel any negative energies seep out of your pores and washing down the drain as the bathtub empties. When you take a shower you can also cleanse energy by feeling any negative energies washing down your body and down the drain.

SALT

Salt is a fantastic cleanser. You can use Epsom salts or rock salt in a bath or a handful of salt as a scrub in the shower. The ocean with its salt water is one of the best cleansers of negative energy. The fresh smell of the ocean can also give you a feeling of being refreshed and restore your energy. When you feel stressed from the hustle and bustle of everyday life, if you can head towards the ocean and take a swim.

CLAPPING

The three-clap technique has been used for many years to remove any form of negativity, including fears, thoughts, images, emotions, external events, and so on. You can also use continuous clapping to check the energy in a room or environment. When your clap is crisp, clear and easy to do, this generally indicates that the energy is light and flowing.

However, when the clap is heavy, dull or flat sounding, there is more than likely stagnant, stuck and/or negative energy within the space. You can clear any negative energy you feel in your environment by staying in the spots where you feel it and continue to clap your hands until you feel the clap become crisper and clearer.

BRUSH

You can also use your hands to brush any negative energy from your energy body. You can do this by standing up and starting from the top of your head using the palms of both hands slowly and gently brush yourself off, working all the way down to your feet. As you do this, your intention and focus should be to feel and know that you are cleansed from all negative energy (including debris, toxins, impurities, energy blockages or lower vibrating energies). Feel and know that these negative energies will flow to the centre of the earth to be transformed into positive, higher, finer, vibrating energy that will be re-used by the Universe at the appropriate time.

MUSIC/SOUND

You can use the sound from a bell, Tibetan singing bowl, clapping (as described above), sticks, drums as well as your own voice to cleanse your energy or the energy within a room. One way in which you can use you own voice is through chanting. 'OM' is a very powerful ancient Sanskrit symbol, sacred syllable and mantra which when chanted can cleanse your own energy as well as the energy in any room.

HERBS & INCENSE

A favourite technique for cleansing is to burn sacred herbs or incense, allowing the energetic properties of the plants to be released and the smoke to waft through your aura or environment to carry away any impurities. Sage is commonly used by Native American healers, shamans and witches in a process called Smudging as they believe that it takes negative energy up to Spirit to be transformed.

There are two main ways in which you can smudge. Firstly, you can use a bundle of dried herbs held together with twine called a smudge stick which is ignited at the end, blown out and allowed to smoulder. When using a smudge stick, often made up of either white sage alone or mixed with other fragrant herbs, it is best to use a large feather to fan the smoke around your energetic field, home or workplace to cleanse the energy. Alternatively, you can light a charcoal block which is placed in a heatproof dish and then add loose dried, semi-powdered herbs or resin onto the charcoal to smoulder. Once lit allow the charcoal disc to turn grey before placing the incense on top. Again use a feather to waft the energies into your auric field and your space. Some of the more common herbs used in cleansing are Sage, Dragon's Blood, Copal, Hyssop, Cedar, Eucalyptus, Rosemary and Lemon. You can also use the following herbs or incense to help clean any negative energies from particular chakras:

- **Base:** Basil, Patchouli, Tea Tree

- **Sacral:** Orange, Jasmine, Ylang-Ylang
- **Solar Plexus:** Lemon, Pine, Sage
- **Heart:** Chamomile, Lavender, Rose
- **Throat:** Eucalyptus, Lemongrass, Peppermint
- **Third Eye:** Geranium, Myrrh. Violet
- **Crown:** Bergamot, Frankincense, Sandalwood

While the energy and fragrance from the herbs pours through your chakra, visualise the smoke as different colours swirling in and around your body, filling you with radiant colour.

ESSENTIAL OILS

Our sense of smell is the most primitive and most closely associated with our emotions and how our body responds to them, so one of the best ways to cleanse yourself of negative energies is through the use of essential oils. You can make a spray from water and aromatherapy oils such as rosemary, lavender or any oil you intuitively feel will help reduce negative energy. You can also place essential oils in a diffuser, anoint yourself or massage them into pressure points on your body to help you cleanse. The following oils can be used with the chakras to help cleanse the specific energy centres:

- **Base:** Ylang-Ylang, Vetiver
- **Sacral:** Cedarwood, Tangerine, Pettigrain, Geranium
- **Solar Plexus:** Bergamot, Grapefruit, Rosemary, Lemongrass
- **Heart:** Eucalyptus, Peppermint, Rosewood

- **Throat:** Geranium, Lemon, Pepper, Sweet Birch
- **Third Eye:** Lavender, Magnolia, Ylang-Ylang
- **Crown:** Frankincense, Gardenia

CRYSTALS

Carrying, wearing or placing crystals on your body or around your home or office can help to cleanse your energy and the environment. The best crystals for cleansing energy include:

- Clear Quartz
- Amethyst
- Chevron Amethyst
- Bloodstone
- Moon Opal
- Citrine

Any of the above crystals can be carried in pouches or worn as jewellery throughout the day or while meditating to help cleanse your energy. You can also place them on your computer screen or around your home and office.

Note: Remember to cleanse your crystals of unwanted vibrations and energies after each use.

AFFIRMATIONS

The simplest way to cleanse your energy is to use your thoughts. To cleanse yourself you can begin by imagining a bright light coming down over your body and say 'I now let go of and release all negative energy from within my aura'. You can also use affirmations in a similar way to cleanse your personal space, the space you work in or any other environment by saying All negative energies and entities are removed from this space. Only love and light are allowed in'. You can say the following affirmations each day to help cleanse your energy:

- I am cleansed of all negative energies
- I release any toxicity from every level of my energy field
- I let go of old beliefs that keep me stuck in old patterns
- I let go of everything I do not want or need for my highest good
- I now release and am released from everything and everybody that is no longer part of the divine plan for my life I now fully and freely release and let go
- I let go and grow
- I let go and trust

VISUALISATION & MEDITATION

Visualisations are a fantastic way to help you cleanse and clear energy from your bodies and/or environment by imagining surroundings, images and situations which represent cleansing and clearing. You can also undertake a similar process to cleanse by going into a meditation where the mind is quiet, your feel relaxed and the body, mind and spirit can be cleared. To help you to cleanse and remove impurities and lower energy as well as clearing various aspects within your energy, listen to my Cleansing and Clearing Energy Meditation.

CHAPTER 6. SPIRITUAL PROTECTION

As you become more sensitive to the energies that constantly surround you, it becomes important to protect your energy field so that you are less susceptible to and not easily upset by any negativity that you may encounter. The more spiritually aware and intuitive you are the more sensitive you become to all the energies around you and need to protect your energy from taking on any unnecessary emotions, fears and problems.

WHAT?

As you start to develop your intuition and spiritual awareness you will become more sensitive to all the energies, positive and/or negative, that constantly surround you. So you need to become consciously aware of protecting your energy in order to avoid picking up and absorbing any negativity or any unnecessary emotions/problems that you may encounter when dealing with other people throughout your daily life.

WHY?

One of the sometime problematic areas of psychic development is the consequential increase in sensitivity to all energies which are flowing within and through you. As you begin working with other people, whether during readings, healings, spiritual counselling etc, you are connecting into their energy or the energy of their loved ones who have passed. When you connect in with this energy you may be exposed to negative energy whether it is thoughts, emotions, beliefs or patterns of behaviour, fear, anger, hatred, depression or negative people/places. Arguments actually create negative energy that can cling to your energy field (aura) or build up in your home and cause problems over time. Also, if someone is thinking or speaking negatively about you, then they are projecting negative energy in your direction. If you experience some of the following, you may need to look at cleansing and then protecting your energy bodies:

- Irritable/losing your temper
- Drained/low energy
- Insomnia/poor sleep habits/nightmares
- Easily influenced by others
- Threatened/defensive
- Fanatical about someone/something
- Feeling other people's emotions/pain
- Bumping into people
- Copying or living your life through others
- Feeling pain in the back of your neck, solar plexus (pit of stomach), or wrists.

Note: Many of these can also be linked to other physical conditions or illnesses, if in doubt always check with your GP.

Therefore, it is important that while you are developing spiritually, you protect yourself from any negative outside influences which could have an impact on your life.

WHEN & WHERE?

Once you have used one of the techniques for grounding and cleansing your energy, it is important to protect and shield the new energy. It is good to get into a routine of protecting and shielding your energy in the mornings when you awake up, and then removing it when you go to bed at night. If you feel you have a lot of activity around you at night, you can also choose to keep your protection on. When you start to feel any of the symptoms of being 'unprotected', it is also important that you protect your energy so that you start to feel calm, in control and have more clarity about your situation. You can protect your energy virtually anywhere, at anytime, whether you feel threatened or not. At night before you go to bed, before leaving the house in the morning, before travelling anywhere, while working, driving, etc., as well as during ritual, or while meditating are the most common times to protect your energy.

How?

There are many different techniques for protecting your energy field. You may need to try a few different techniques or adapt them to suit your own needs and what you feel comfortable with. While it is impossible to cover all of them, a few different techniques are provided below so that you can start trying some of these techniques to see which one(s) work best for you. Where energy is particularly negative or heavy, you may want to double your protection by using two or more of the below methods.

MANDALAS

Mandala is the Sanskrit word for circle or whole world, representing protection, good luck, healing, or completion. They are a visual representation of the Universe and everything within it which uses geometric shapes and are contemplated during meditation. For centuries, mandalas have been used by Native American's in healing rituals, Tibetan paintings, Gothic rose windows, labyrinths within Cathedrals and Hindu yantras. A psychic mandala is used to bring in positive energy and eliminate negativity. You can design your own mandala by incorporating various shapes such as angles, triangles, squares, rectangles, circles or symbols as well as colours which characterise protection for you. You can create your own protective mandala for your home or any other environment using the following ritual:

Cleanse the space you wish to protect

Go outside and find a stick for each entry

Give thanks to Mother Earth for allowing you to remove the sticks

Bring the sticks to your altar (if you have one) and then light a white candle

Anoint the sticks with geranium, garlic or rosemary oil while focusing on placing protective energy into the sticks

Take each stick and place them near all entrances with the intention
of protecting the space

Give thanks and gratitude to the Angels, Spirit and Mother Earth for
helping to protect the space

You can repeat this ritual when the sticks no longer smell.

SYMBOLS

Many cultures have specific symbols they use for protection, warding off evil and bringing in positive energy. Symbols are very personal and should only be worn or carried if they feel right and comfortable for you. The following are some of the more common symbols used for protection:

The **pentagram**, a five-pointed star, protects against witchcraft and the evil eye, visible and invisible spiritual attacks and returns negative energy back to the sender.

Celtic Knots protect against plots against you, group magic, evil spirits and demons.

The **Celtic Cross** is thought to protect from spiritual dangers of all kinds.

Eye of Horus is an important protective symbol in ancient Egypt and helps protect against the evil eye.

The **Pentagram** has five points, representing Spirit and the four elements of earth, air, fire, and water and is associated with as above, so below. It is a powerful protector against evil which shields the wearer and the home against all forms of negativity.

Colour

Colours have been used in religious and mystical groups to denote different hierarchies or levels of authority for many centuries. The following colours are particularly good for protection and can be worn or placed on your physical body or you can visualise yourself surrounded by a bubble or mist of the relevant colour:

- Gold is associated with the sun and carries a powerful positive energy (Yang). Therefore, it removes any energy that is not in harmony with it. This colour is most beneficial in situations where the energy is particularly dense or disturbing.

- White is a good protective colour for normal day-to-day circumstances as it symbolises purity and vitality. It reflects back whatever is sent at it so it is useful when someone is sending negative energy your way because it allows them to see how their thoughts and actions have affected you.

- Sky-blue carries the quality of spiritual love. A soothing, passive energy that neutralises and harmonises what is projected onto it. This colour is useful to transform and diffuse negative energies in a non-intrusive and gentle way.

- Pink represents unconditional love and protects you from any negative energy.

- Black is not a colour, but rather the lack of colour, so it is useful when you do not want to be noticed because it can be used to create invisibility. It is particularly useful for protection if you are extremely sensitive to picking up other people's energy or energy within your environment. It wards off hatred and negative emotions and should be used in combination with other colours

These are some of the main colours that people use for protection; however, you can use other colours that intuitively appeal to you. Experiment with different colours and noting down what you feel or sense about these qualities to find out what works for you.

HERBS

Plants and herbs have been used for thousands of years by those who perform rituals to awaken psychic abilities, clear homes and people of negative vibrations, attract love, money, luck, deepens spirituality, for protection and much more. Herbs can be added to incense and oils to increase their energies, used to dress candles or in special blend potpourri. You can fill some dishes with protective plants or herbs which are good for preventing (and removing) negative energy such as aloe, anise, basil, cactus, carnation, cedar, chamomile, cinnamon, cumin, curry, dill, dragon's blood, eucalyptus, fennel, fern, flax, frankincense, garlic, ginseng, ivy, lavender, myrrh, onion, parsley, pepper, peppermint, rosemary, sage, thyme. Then place these dishes on tables or shelves in the main parts of your home. You can also make pretty herbal sachets or "charm bags" to hang on doors, tuck in a drawer or place in your car for protection while travelling. Sprinkle protective herbs on the tops of doorways, or at the thresholds of your home.

Note: Some herbs are toxic and should be kept well out of reach of children and animals. The herbs should also be replaced every few months, but sprinkle the old herbs outside so that they can be returned to the earth.

ANGELS & SPIRIT GUIDES

One of the most effective ways to protect yourself from negative energies as you are developing spiritually is to ask for protection from your Angels and Spirit Guides. You do not walk alone in this life, you are always surrounded by Angels and Spirit Guides who guide you and protect you on   your journey. From the moment you were born you were 'assigned Angels and Guides, who's 'job' it is to protect you, comfort and guide you, and   to work with you to ensure that you live the most productive life possible here on earth. Your Angels and Guides must be invited to help you as they cannot interfere with your free will. So you can ask them for their protection for general purposes, or you can ask when you have   an immediate need. Please remember the Angels and Guides are not your slaves, they help you because they want to, so please respect and be grateful when requesting their assistance. Be thankful for their presence in your life and know that you are never alone.

Stand or sit down in a comfortable location where you will not be interrupted.

Take two or three deep breaths in and out until you feel relaxed.

Then request in your mind or out loud one (or more) of the following:

Archangel Raphael stands before me and protects me from all harm.

Archangel Michael stands to the right of me and protects me from all harm

Archangel Gabriel stands behind me and protects me from all harm

Archangel Uriel stands to the left of me and protects me from all harm

CRYSTALS

Crystals have been used since the time of the Ancient Egyptians as certain crystals carry natural protective qualities. You can place specific crystals in the corners of a room at home or in the office, carry, wear or place crystals on your body to act as a shield from negative energies. The best crystals for protecting energy include:

- Amethyst
- Black Obsidian
- Blue Aventurine
- Carnelian
- Citrine
- Garnet
- Kyanite
- Lapis Lazuli
- Mookaite

Any of the above crystals can be carried in pouches or worn as jewellery throughout the day or while meditating to help protect your energy. You can also place them on the four corners of a table that you are working from.

Note: Remember to cleanse your crystals of unwanted vibrations and energies after each use.

SPIRITUAL BOUNDARIES

One of the most important things to learn when first opening up and developing spiritually is to claim your power and protect yourself by setting strong, healthy personal and spiritual boundaries. Boundaries are personal guidelines or limits about what you are prepared to accept in your relationships and from people (living or passed) and can be physical, mental, emotional or spiritual. They are also tools you can use to resist negative and to accept support and nurturing from others. Boundaries help you to be able to bring order to your life and as you learn to strengthen your boundaries, you gain a clearer sense of yourself and your relationship to others. Boundaries empower you to determine how you will be treated by others. They are invisible and symbolic 'fences' that help to protect you from negative energies. For further details about spiritual boundaries refer to chapter 7.

LIVING YOUR TRUTH

The best form of psychic protection is to live your truth. What is your divine purpose? Find it. Then actually live it. If you are doing what you are meant to be doing, the Universe will support you and there is very little anyone else can do or say that will be able to stop you. Your truth is not your destiny. You must choose to fulfil it, and once you choose to consciously live your full purpose, you will have a divine protection that will help you in all of life's difficult areas.

AFFIRMATIONS

Because what we feel and think creates energy, affecting us and the people around us in the most subtle of ways, being positive and honestly knowing yourself is one of the strongest protections you have against negative energy. Positive energies dissolve or 'cancel out' negative ones, so you can direct a positive thought of the same, or greater, strength at any negative thought. The following affirmations can be used each day, or when you feel drawn, to spiritually protect your energy:

1. I am surrounded by pure divine white light, protecting me from any and all negativity, danger and harm
2. I am divinely protected and cared for
3. I feel safe, secure and protected
4. I know I am safe and Spirit continually watches over me
5. I live in a protected and safe environment

You can also arrange for positive spirits to help protect you against negative ones.

VISUALISATION & MEDITATION

Rather than focusing on an external object, you can use visualisations to focus on the internal and image that you are safe and protected in your surroundings, situations or everyday life. Meditation is also a great way to help you relax, rejuvenate the body, mind and spirit through a process of deep relaxation and then protect your energy. Listen to my Energy Protection Meditation to help you to protect your energy or your space from negative energies.

Again, while there are many different ways to protect and shield your energy, it is important to make sure that your shield does not have any holes or gaps from which your energy can be drained. Your protection should feel so comfortable, you should be able to just know it is there as part of you. With lots of practice and regular protecting you will find that you will build up a strong shield of protection that is with you always.

CHAPTER 7. SPIRITUAL BOUNDARIES

One of the most important things to learn when first opening up and developing spiritually is to claim your power and protect yourself by setting strong, healthy personal and spiritual boundaries. Boundaries are personal guidelines or limits about what you are prepared to accept in your relationships and from people (living or passed) and can be physical, mental, emotional or spiritual. They are also tools you can use to resist negative and to accept support and nurturing from others. Boundaries help you to be able to bring order to your life and as you learn to strengthen your boundaries, you gain a clearer sense of yourself and your relationship to others. Boundaries empower you to determine how you will be treated by others. They are invisible and symbolic 'fences 'that have three main purposes:

1. to keep people from coming into your space and mistreating you
2. to keep you from going into the space of others and mistreating them
3. to enable you to embody your sense of 'who you are'

Your skin is the most intimate boundary you possess because it literally establishes where you end and everything else begins.

Physical Boundaries

Everything inside your skin is you and everything outside is not you. So, your sense of personal space is a significant part of your physical boundary and determines how close you will allow others to come to you. They represent your level of personal comfort, sexual expression and privacy and help you to recognise who you are ok to be touched by, as well as how, when and where. For example, some of you might be open to hugging everyone that you meet while others may have a hard time just shaking hands. Other physical boundaries may involve clothes, shelter, safety, money, time, etc. For example, some of you may keep your doors open (even unlocked) while others like the curtains drawn. While most physical boundaries are comforting they can also be quite limiting and end upholding you back from moving forward in life.

Mental & Emotional Boundaries

Mental and emotional boundaries which include your values, beliefs, thoughts, ideas, feelings, decisions, interests, relationships, responsibilities, respect and so on are also important.

Core Values

To understand the boundaries you want to set for yourself, you must know who you truly are and what you do on a daily basis, which is defined by your core values. Your core values are non- negotiable, consistent, truly important to you and energise and affect all areas of your life. Whether you are consciously aware of them or not, you all have and demonstrate your core values by the way you live your life. Your values are about what you need in order to live your life authentically so that you can be happy and feel good. These are about your firmly held beliefs about what makes you a person of value and also what you see as valuable in others. Most people never define their core values because it requires a lot of reflection which makes establishing boundaries extremely difficult. Some common core values include:

- Authenticity
- Integrity
- Influence
- Happiness
- Peace
- Wealth
- Love
- Power
- Success
- Friendship
- Family
- Justice
- Status
- Joy
- Wisdom

- Recognition

When you are aligned with your deeply held core values, you are being true to and honouring yourself, resulting in a sense of fulfilment, well-being and satisfaction. You also energise yourself and those around you, move forward in the right direction, attract people with similar values, successfully create and sustain meaningful relationships and create greater unity among family, friends, clients, employees etc. Your boundaries are tied to and work together with your values as they allow you to know what is good and bad, and right and wrong, both in terms of morals and how you feel about what is going on around you. So if you have strong values which align with your actions then you have strong boundaries in place to support your values. However, where you have little or no boundaries, your values may be superficial or weak and cause stress and other not so positive impacts on your life.

BELIEFS

Your true identity is also built around what you decide you are going to believe, which then shapes your daily actions, thoughts and choices. Beliefs are your individual truths, your rules for living, and your view of the way life is and the way it should be. They are your thoughts about yourself, about others, about how you expect things to be, how you think things really are, what you think is really true and what consequences you expect are likely to follow from particular behaviour. Your beliefs are normally developed over time, are what you have grown up with and have 'learnt' to believe and act upon which therefore gives you a sense of certainty and a basis for decision-making. Beliefs can be empowering, related to excellence and how it could be achieved, or limiting where your behaviour is not what you want, but you think you cannot change it.

When you are in direct alignment with your beliefs, hold them to be true and act upon them, you feel strong and empowered and create strong boundaries that protect you and align yourself with people who hold similar beliefs. If you are out of alignment with your beliefs and not acting on them, you can keep yourself locked behind your fears which often results in anger. Therefore, it is important to ensure that you are in direct alignment with your values.

EMOTIONS

Emotional boundaries define where your feelings end and another person's begins. To create healthy boundaries it is extremely important to connect with your feelings. Your emotional boundaries are often created by the response you receive in certain situations. If you were encouraged to talk about and identify your feelings and they were dealt with warmly and lovingly, you more than likely have a strong sense of your emotional boundaries. However, if you have learnt to push your emotions away, separate yourself from your feelings and to ignore them because your feelings have been met with disapproval, harshness or simply ignored in the past, you probably need to set some emotional boundaries. The following questions may help you to identify if you have strong or weak emotional boundaries:

- Do you take responsibility for your feelings and needs, and allow others to do the same?
- Do you feel overly responsible for the feelings and needs of others and neglect your own?
- Are you able to say 'no'?
- Can you ask for what you need?
- Are you a compulsive people pleaser?
- Do you become upset simply because others are upset around you?
- Do you mimic the opinions of whoever you are around?

Sometimes protection, particularly from people who are harmful to you, intentionally or unintentionally, is as simple as saying 'no' and sticking to it. If someone asks you to do something or go somewhere, and you only say yes because you are afraid of being 'mean' or 'letting them down' but you know it's not a good situation for you, you must learn to say no. As an adult, only you define what is acceptable and unacceptable in your life. Draw those boundaries and stick to them.

SPIRITUAL BOUNDARIES

As you begin to develop spiritually, it is extremely important that you establish spiritual boundaries. Spiritual boundaries relate to religion, spiritual practices and your connection to your Inner Self, Higher Self and Spirit. You and you alone choose a spiritual path for yourselves. Others may help and assist you on your path however no one can force you to take a particular pathway because your spiritual development comes from within yourself.

VIOLATIONS OF BOUNDARIES

PHYSICAL

The most common way in which physical boundaries can be violated is through inappropriate or unwanted touch or the absence of touch which may result in you creating rigid boundaries, perhaps walls. You might also have physical boundaries which are not solid and not know that you have the right to say 'no' and end up with your boundaries violated. Below are some common examples of violations of physical boundaries:

- Standing too close to a person without their permission
- Touching a person (physically or sexually) without their permission
- Getting into a person's personal belongings and living space (eg. Wallet, mail, wardrobe).

133

- Listening to a person's personal conversations or telephone calls without their permission
- Not allowing a person to have privacy or violating a person's right to privacy

MENTAL & EMOTIONAL

Some common examples how behaviour does not align with your values and indicate little or a lack of boundaries include:

- Make a commitment or promise to do something but fail to follow through, which reveals a lack of integrity
- Yelling, screaming and verbally abusing others, calling people names, ridiculing or patronising people, which reveals a lack of respect
- Telling someone how they should be or what they should do, which reveals negative issues with control

When any of your beliefs are challenged, your immediate response is to resist which may even turn to anger if you find it personally insulting. One of the most common ways that your beliefs may be violated is when others tell you what you 'should' believe. For example, if you believe in life after death, your belief may be challenged by others and you may feel like you are being personally attacked for your belief. So it is important to identify any limiting beliefs that may be holding you back and change, replace or discard them completely. Listed below are some unhealthy beliefs which you may be familiar with that allow boundaries to be ignored or violated:

- I can never say 'no' to others
- I can never trust anyone again
- I would feel guilty if I did something on my own
- I should do everything I can to spend as much time together with you
- If I keep quiet and do not complain people will eventually leave me alone
- As long as I am not seen or heard, I will not be violated or hurt
- I would rather not pay attention to what is happening to me in this relationship, so I do not have to feel the pain and hurt
- I have been hurt badly in the past and I will never let anyone in close enough to hurt me again

When you ignore, push away or separate yourself from how you're feeling as a result of other's actions or allow others to hurt you emotionally, they are not affected. So you need to draw a limit between the two of you, letting them know that they have violated one of your emotional boundaries. Emotional boundaries can be violated through:

- Words or actions which reduce your sense of self-esteem, self-worth and ability to function as a valuable member of the community
- Words or actions which reduce your sense of self-esteem, self-worth and ability to function as available member of the community

- Unclear roles (child forced to take on parent role)
- Disrespectful behaviour
- Name-calling
- Foul language
- Belittling
- Refusing to acknowledge your needs, wants or you as a person Having opinions and ideas dismissed or ignored

SPIRITUAL

If a spirit has violated your boundaries and blended with your energy at an inappropriate time/place or is making you feel uncomfortable, then they are violating your spiritual boundaries. Some common physical symptoms you may experience if a spirit blends too closely include:

- Sudden headache
- Dizziness
- Clenching your jaw
- Heart racing, blood pumping in your ears
- Chills, cold-like symptoms
- Feeling inexplicably nervous, frantic or panicked Sore neck, sore back

IGNORED BOUNDARIES

You can tell boundaries are being ignored if one or more of the following signs are evident:

EXCESSIVE DETACHMENT

When you and others in a group or family are totally independent, have no emotional connection, lack a common purpose, goal, identity, or rationale for existing together. You and the other people do not have any desire to come together and form a union out of fear that you will lose your personal identities.

OVER ENMESHMENT

When you and everyone in a group have to think, feel, and act in the same way, without deviation from the norms. Uniqueness and autonomy are not considered acceptable.

DISASSOCIATION

When you are exposed to a stressful emotional event, you may blank out and loose touch with your feelings about what happened and be unable to remember. When you feel your physical and/or emotional space is being violated you tell yourself 'it does not matter', 'ignore it and it will go away', 'don't fight it, just hang on and it will be over soon', 'do not put up a struggle or it will be worse'.

VICTIMHOOD OR MARTYRDOM

When you feel someone has violated or disrespected one of your boundaries, you may feel discounted, hurt, oppressed, ignored, abused, or taken advantage of. Your slogan is 'poor me' and you may actively or passively encourage others to victimise you as a means of gaining love or attention and then let others know of your martyrdom (suffering).

PERSECUTOR OR RESCUER

When you subtly or obviously tell others they are not good enough, or that you are better than them, physically or emotionally abuse others or limit, blame and oppress others you are persecuting others and violating or disrespecting their boundaries. Also, when you put others needs first, protecting, advising and carrying feelings for them, you violate or disrespect others' boundaries. The rescuer feels responsible for others, thinks they know better than the other person about what they need and say things like 'here, let me do it for you, you poor thing' which places the other person in the victim role and feeling weak or incapable of doing things for themselves. By violating or disrespecting others boundaries you are simply searching for love in a roundabout way.

CHIP ON THE SHOULDER

When you feel angry about violations of physical and/or emotional boundaries or where others have ignored your rights in the past, whether real or perceived, you may have a chip on your shoulder that dares people to come too close to you.

INVISIBILITY

When you don't want others to know how you are really feeling or what you are really thinking, you may withdraw inward or try to over-control so that you are not seen or heard and your boundaries can't be violated.

ALOOFNESS OR SHYNESS

When you have had real or perceived experiences of being ignored, loved or rejected in the past, you become insecure and defend yourself by rejecting others before they reject you. This keeps you focusing inward and results in you being unwilling or fearful of opening up to others.

COLD & DISTANT

When you experience hurt or pain from being violated, hurt, ignored or rejected in the past, a way to keep others out and put them off, you may build walls to make sure that others can't invade your emotional or physical space.

SMOTHERING

When someone is overly concerned about your needs and interests and invades your emotional and physical space, you may feel overwhelmed, like you are being strangled, held too tightly, and lack freedom to breathe.

PRIVACY

When you are expected to let others know all the details about how you feel, reactions, opinions, relationships and dealings with the outside world, you may feel like nothing you think, feel or experience is private.

SETTING HEALTHY BOUNDARIES

When you are not solid with your boundaries, you are vulnerable to emotional pain and lack of authenticity, so it is important to be clear about what your boundaries are in order to protect yourself and so that you know how to respect others boundaries as well. Setting boundaries is not about you controlling other people; it is about deciding what is acceptable and unacceptable for you and then taking steps to do what you can to keep those behaviours that you find unacceptable out of your life. Healthy boundaries need to start from the inside – from you – and while they may take some time, it is never too late to establish healthy boundaries for yourself. You can start now by:

- Identifying how your opinions or values differ from others around you
- Identifying any violations you have experienced, particularly growing up and throughout your childhood, who was involved, any damage caused, forgive it and let it go
- Examining the boundaries established in your relationships and determining if you are comfortable with them or if you need to respectfully re-establish your boundaries.

PHYSICAL

In terms of your physical boundaries, it is important for you to identify and establish boundaries around how close people get to you and the level of physical contact you feel comfortable with. You can begin examining your physical boundaries by answering the following questions to find out what you are comfortable with:

- How close would you allow someone to stand within your personal space before you felt uncomfortable?
- Does it feel ok for you if a stranger places their hand on your shoulder?
- Is it ok for you to allow others to touch you inappropriately?
- Would it be comfortable for a stranger to ask you about your sexual experiences?   I sit ok for you if a stranger walks into your home and they make themselves comfortable without being invited?

Once you have identified all of your values in terms of your physical boundaries, you will then feel more confident in standing in your power and protecting your boundary by speaking up for yourself when and if they are violated or ignored, whether by a person who is living or passed.

MENTAL & EMOTIONAL

The following are some healthier more empowering beliefs which help to reinforce strong boundaries:

- I can say 'no' to others if it invades my space or does not feel right for me
- I can protect myself by assertively speaking up for myself to ensure I am not hurt if my space or rights are violated or ignored
- I explore my own interests and hobbies so that I am my true unique self
- I will stand up for myself and assert my rights to be respected
- If others do not respect my boundaries, then I have the right to leave them or ask them to move out of my life I have a right to be seen and heard
- I choose to open myself up to others trusting that I will be assertive to protect myself and my boundaries

Emotional boundaries define where our feelings end and another person's begin. So you can start examining where your emotional boundaries are by asking yourself the following questions:

- Do you take responsibility for your feelings and needs, and allow others to do the same?
- Do you feel overly responsible for the feelings and needs of others   and neglect our own?
- Are you able to say 'no'?
- Can you ask for what you need?
- Are you a compulsive people pleaser?

- Do you become upset simply because others are upset around you?
- Do you copy the opinions of who you are around?

The answers to the above questions will help you to define where your lines are in terms of your emotional boundaries.

SPIRITUAL

If you notice spirits blending too closely with your energy, the best thing to do is acknowledge it and consciously tell them to step back or say to yourself I'm letting this energy go. Any communication with those in the Spirit world should be completed through your Spirit Guide and is a two way communication process. Therefore, it is important for you to identify what you are and are not comfortable working with spiritually. For example, some people will only feel comfortable working with spirits who are of lighter, higher energetic frequencies. Others feel comfortable working with lower, negative energies to help them cross-over into the light by undertaking spirit rescue work. Once you know what form of spiritual work you are comfortable with and what your boundaries are in terms of when and where spirits can communicate with you, it is important to let your Guides know about these boundaries.

Some final tips for setting healthy boundaries have been included below:

- Set simple clear boundaries in a calm, firm, respectful and loving way without justifying, apologising or rationalising them
- You are responsible for communicating your boundaries and not for other person's reaction to the boundary you are setting
- You have the right to take care of yourself and setting boundaries without feeling anxious, selfish, guilty, or embarrassed takes practice and determination
- Listen to your intuition, if something doesn't feel right than be confident and assertive in setting healthy boundaries with others, so that you no longer have to put up walls
- If you find yourself in the victim role, change your own behaviour by thinking about your boundaries and what you need to do to enforce them
- Ask people to stop doing something hurtful or offensive, ask them to let you figure things out for yourself, or leave (or avoid) a dangerous or toxic situation
- Spend less time with friends or relatives who do not support you Acknowledge and respect other person's responsibility for their own life choices and show empathy, encouragement and confront kindly where you need to
- Offer help if they ask for it and you are willing to give it.

- Your boundaries may be tested, plan on it, expect it, but be firm, clear, and respectful with setting your boundaries
- Make sure your behaviour matches the boundaries you have set up or you will be sending out mixed messages
- Be prepared to stand firm when your boundaries are not respected. Some people will not be willing to respect your boundaries so you may need to put up a wall by ending the relationship
- Setting boundaries is a process which takes time and will be done when you are ready, not when someone else tells you to
- Setting healthy boundaries allows your true self to emerge - and what an exciting journey that is.

CHAPTER 8. CONNECTING TO SPIRIT

Everyone has the capability of connecting energetically with Spirit whether to communicate with your Guides or loved ones who have passed to the spirit world. It is a matter of opening to the energy, via your crown chakra, and connecting. Just like a telephone line up to the heart of the Universe while being connected to Mother Earth via the base chakra or the soles of your feet. Because the energy in the world of spirit is vibrating at different, higher rates from that of the physical world, you need to open up to Divine energy, raise your spiritual vibrations, sit in the power of Spirit and then blend your energy with that of Spirit so that information can be sent and received.

RAISING VIBRATION & BUILDING SPIRITUAL POWER

When you raise your spiritual vibration, you begin to resonate at a higher frequency which increases your awareness and connection with Spirit. When you feel "low" or "down" your spiritual vibration would be low, however, when you feel "up" or "high" you have a high vibration. To consciously connect with Spirit, you have to be in this 'higher' state of vibration. Some examples of how you can raise your spiritual vibration include:

- Purifying your body (eat fresh fruits and vegetables, whole grains, nuts etc as well as drink plenty of water)
- Exercise (from running to yoga to rock climbing, exercise will rev up your energy)
- Focus on positive thoughts and emotions ('low' feelings include anger, sorrow, guilt, hatred, despair, fear, jealousy and frustration whereas 'up' feelings include respect, appreciation, joy, hope, strength, peace, love)
- Surround yourself with uplifting, positive people, or with a beautiful,   peaceful or happy environment
- Meditate (quiet your mind, focus on your breathing and listen)
- Practice gratitude and compassion (remember how blessed you are   and help someone less fortunate than you) Journal to explore your own personal growth

Meditation is one of the best ways to help raise your vibration. As you begin to vibrate at a higher frequency you will increase your awareness and your connection with Spirit. Meditation will help you to clear your mind, help you find your spiritual path and gain clarity on some of your questions. No doubt you have been taught many different techniques for how to meditate. While I believe that each of you will find a method that works best for you, it is important to remember that the intention is always to clear your mind, let go of all earthly thoughts and to simply sit and be at One with Spirit. When you sit at One with Spirit you are building your spiritual power (raising your vibration). You are not seeking answers or solutions to any problems you may be experiencing. The purpose is to simply increase your vibration so that you are able to connect with those in the spirit world with ease and grace. Please don't skip right over it. Being conscious of your breathing and your connection with Spirit--even if it is just for a few moments--will make a huge difference in your day. Simply breathe in Spirit, and exhale whatever you would like to release (fear, anger, pain, etc.) This is a practice you must do for ten minutes each day, longer if possible, at a regular time so that Spirit will be there to help you build your energy. By building your spiritual power every day, you are also reminding yourself of your constant connection with Spirit, which will free you to receive the gifts that are being offered to you. Listen to my Sitting in the Power with Spirit Meditation to support you in your personal and spiritual development by allowing you to raise your vibration to meet and connect with those in the Spirit World by Sitting in the Power with Spirit in order to receive their energy for your own learn, growth and development.

INTUITION V'S EGO (FEAR)

Intuition means instinctive and unconscious knowing without deduction or reasoning. Intuitive guidance will appear quickly, like a lightning bolt, often in response to a question or a request for support and help and feel light, positive, motivating and encouraging. These types of messages will consistently and repetitively appear over and over again, almost always motivated by a desire to improve a situation and will urge you to continue forwards with a 'you can do it' feeling behind them. Intuitive information will also fit with your natural talents, skills, abilities, passions and interests, will always come from a high vibrational space of love, joy, happiness and will move you forwards on your journey.

Ego based guidance often comes in very slowly in response to worry and/or fear (false evidence appearing real), is inconsistent, disorganised, shreds your confidence, and aims to make you rich, famous and place you above others. This type of information will often contain advice or actions to take which hold absolutely no interest or desire for you to follow, keep you stuck in situations which do not serve your highest good and comes from a negative vibrational space.

Therefore, when you first begin working with Spirit it is extremely important to be able to recognise the difference between guidance which is received intuitively versus that from fear (ego). The more you are able to recognise true intuitive guidance the more you will begin to trust the information you are given and Spirit to guide you along your path towards success.

CONNECTING & BLENDING WITH SPIRIT

Once you have lifted your vibration and built up your spiritual energy, the next step is to connect and blend with those in the Spirit world. Before doing any spiritual work it is obviously important to connect to Spirit before you begin. You have probably been taught, shown or read about many different methods for connecting with Spirit, including opening all of your chakra's from the base chakra up to your crown etc etc etc. Yes you need to calm your mind, building your spiritual power (raising your vibration) so you are closer to Spirit and be receptive to being able to sense and have contact with Spirit. However, connecting is as easy as acknowledging that you already have a connection with Spirit.

Those in the Spirit world are beings of energy and light, so when you want to sense and have contact with Spirit, invite them to connect with you and they will then attempt to blend their spiritual energies with yours. Because your spiritual vibration is much slower than that of Spirit, if you have increased your spiritual vibration Spirit can meet you half way between their normal vibration and your own normal vibration so that communication is possible. To blend with those in the Spirit world you simply need to invite them to step in closer so that you can blend with their energy and begin to work with them. You are normally more receptive to contact from the Spirit world as you fall to sleep and just before you wake up, while you are daydreaming or in a meditative state because your mind is calm and not filled with thoughts about your every-day life. So, once a spirit steps in closer, you will sense them in your energy field, can get out of your own way and begin to 'link in' with the spirit so that you can eventually pass on messages to their loved ones.

Spirit Guides

Just as you are a spiritual being in a physical body, guides are spiritual beings who do not have bodies at this time. But they have probably had physical bodies before and they might even have bodies again. You will often hear Spiritual workers, mediums and psychics refer to Spirit Guides, however, please do not get hung up on what your guide looks like, where they are from etc. Most spirits (including Guides) make themselves known to you in some human (or animal) like 'form' to make it easy for you to identify them rather than their true 'spirit light' image. For example, a guide might look like a Red Indian, Chinese person, Eagle, Crow etc. Guides are none of these things because Spirit is spirit (light). They usually look the same whenever you see them otherwise you would get confused and think you have hundreds of guides. The most important thing, is knowing that you have guides, feeling their energy and understanding how to work with them.

MAIN GUIDE OR GUARDIAN OR GUARDIAN ANGEL

This is the most enlightened and important spirit helping to look after you as an individual. They are responsible for protecting us when we intentionally, or unintentionally, leave our bodies (Astral Travel etc) and providing us with overall spiritual guidance and are usually with you for the whole of your physical life. As they have access to the 'akashic record' or 'Book of Life', they are able to remind us of our past lives.

Your main guide will be there to help you when you cross into the Spirit World.

GUIDES

There are other guides who are not usually with us all the time but come in when they are able to help guide you or learn something new. These spirits have often known us in this and/or a previous life/lives as a brother, sister, wife, husband etc and will tend to be of a similar spiritual age to you, 'like attracts like'.

HELPERS

These spirits are like guides, but they often share the same interest as us and are simply interested in what you are doing. For example, if you are a dancer, and a spirit who was a dancer is aware that you are dancing, they may come close to you so that they can feel what you are doing.

GATEKEEPER OR DOORKEEPER

Mediums or people who channel Spirit by getting in and out of their physical bodies use a gatekeeper or doorkeeper guide. If you do a form of mediumship (channelling) that involves you getting in and out of your physical body then a spirit is often appointed to help you get in and out safely and to stop other spirits taking over your physical bodies ('possession).

Your spirit guide watches over you and offers guidance and support on your spiritual journey--even if you're not aware of it. A true spirit guide is an evolved being who has agreed to support your spiritual evolution. True spirit guides are wise, compassionate and often amusing as well as respect you and your right to choose your own path. If you are ever aware of a spiritual being who does not respect you and others, it is not your spirit guide, and you need to tell them to 'back-off' and call in your real guide.

RECEIVING INFORMATION

The key to communicating with and receiving information from Spirit is to be aware of the language used. Spirit communicates with us in two different ways, externally and internally. Firstly, external communication comes in the forms of signs such as finding feathers, coins etc and synchronicities where you tap into the flow of Spirit and the right people and opportunities flow into your life at just the right time. Another way that Spirit communicates with us is through internal communication, where information from spirit is delivered through your heightened physical senses, known as the 'Clairs'.

CLAIRVOYANCE

Clairvoyance is the ability to 'see' visions and is commonly known as 'clear seeing'. This means that you are able to see with the mind's eye; people, spirits, places or objects, colours, symbols etc. These visions can be experiences on a physical level, however, are often flashed into the medium's mind so that they can be described during a reading or when giving a message. You may also start catching glimpses of spirit out of the corner of your eye, see the colours in people's auras, or sometimes you may see spirits as tiny sparks of light, transparent orbs or beads, shadows or a normal figure standing or moving to one side.

CLAIRAUDIENCE

Clairaudience is essentially 'clear hearing'. This means that you are able to hear sounds or words, either on a physical level or as a voice in your head, from those in the Spirit world, whether that is your own Spirit Guide or someone's loved one who has passed over. These sounds or words will normally come to you quickly, for example; names, dates and places etc.

CLAIRSENTIENCE

Clairsentience is 'clear feeling' or 'clear sensing'. This means that you are able to feel for information from Spirit in a number of different ways. This can be experienced as:

1. a 'gut feeling', that is a strong emotional response that feels almost physical
2. 'empathy', that is pick up on other people's feelings and put yourself in their shoes
3. physical sensations, that is sensations within your own body to let you know about physical appearance, health conditions, personality

CLAIRGUSTANCE

Clairgustance is 'clear tasting'. This means that you are able to recognize different substances, ingredients etc from Spirit through your sense of taste.

CLAIRSCENT

Clairscent is essentially 'clear smelling'. This means that you are able to smell a fragrance or odour coming from Spirit. These smells are often experienced on a physical level as a reminder that a passed loved one is close to us.

While one of your senses may be more dominant than the others, it is important not to expect that information from Spirit will be delivered in the same way each time as this blocks the many other, and often easier, ways that Spirit has available for you to receive information. So be open to communicating with and receiving information from Spirit in a variety of ways.

TRUST V'S FEAR & DOUBT

DOUBT

Doubt is 'a feeling of uncertainty about the truth' (Webster's dictionary). Because our brains are only capable of focusing on one thing at a time, in the physical world, when you have a negative thought, you immediately put up a wall and block out positive feelings from coming into your mind. You can become more conscious of when doubt or a negative thought comes into your mind and simply replace it with a more positive one. Doubt works the same way with Spirit. Once Spirit blends with your energy if you begin to doubt you abilities, you become uncertain about the information given to you or you have a negative thought (I can't do this) you immediately block Spirit from blending and working with you. If doubt comes in, you will need to work harder to re-establish the connection with Spirit and simply stick to the facts you are being given.

FEAR

If you see, hear or sense Spirits and you become fearful this could be stopping you from moving forward with your Mediumship. To conquer your fear, you must be brave and learn to trust that the reason you see and feel these things is because you have a GIFT for doing so. You can reduce fear of the spirit world, by educating, informing and preparing yourself so that you can quickly become more in control of HOW and WHEN you receive information. If you are seeing, hearing or sensing too much, then talk to your Spirit Guides and let them know that you are not comfortable and ask them to slow things down and give it to you at a pace you are more comfortable with. You can also let your guides know that you would like to set up boundaries around when Spirits can connect and blend with you so that you are not surprised and you are consciously aware of what is happening. You are in control. You can make a Spirit clearer, or less intense, tune them out, ignore them, tell them to go away etc. Nothing should enter your energy field without your permission. The only time Spirit can enter your space and your energy, is when you forget that you are in charge and you are too fearful of telling them to get out of your space, or when you have not consciously set boundaries around how you wish to work with Spirit. You can also overcome fear by communicating with Spirit more often. However, if you ever get into a position where you do not feel like you can control what you are seeing, hearing or sensing, then ask someone for help, don't try to deal with it on your own.

TRUST

It is important to be aware that in order for a mediumship reading to be effective there must be a level of trust and a cooperative relationship between the medium and the person in Spirit. According to author Stephen M. R. Covey, "...Trust is based on principles of empowerment, reciprocity, and fundamental belief that most people are capable of being trusted...". In the physical world, healthy relationships require a solid foundation of trust which takes confidence, practice and patience on your part. Connecting and blending with Spirit is no different. Once Spirit blends with your energy and steps in closer to begin working with you, it is your responsibility to build trust with them by accurately and truthfully passing on each piece of information they give you. As you begin to pass on the information (without doubting or judging) you are given, the spirit will begin to draw closer to you and start working with you more as you have demonstrated that you are capable of being trusted.

To some of you, the process of connecting and blending with Spirit will come naturally, as you are easily able to quieten your thoughts, get out of your own way and trust the information that Spirit is providing you. For others, fear of getting the information wrong or doubts about your own abilities or the information you are being given, can make this process more difficult. Once you start regularly connecting, blending and communicating with Spirit, it will become easier to step out of your own way so that you can establish a strong connection and trust the information you are being given by Spirit.

While you can't control how other people react to anything you say or do, you can control how their reactions affect you. If you are grounded, you won't be swayed unduly by their reactions. If you are centered, you will be able to respond in a clear and focused way. If you are well protected, anything that is negative won't get into your being and make you want to react. If your aura isn't cluttered with other people's energy, your response will be based in your own truth, not a whole lot of responses you have been taught by others. Taking control of your energy body is the first step to taking back control of your own mind and emotions. It is also one of the first steps to claiming your power as a healer or worker of magic, or indeed as an individual.

Other Books By Leanne, The Barefoot Medium®

Psychic Development: Divination Tools and Techniques

This book provides easy and practical techniques to help you understand more about your intuition, different tools that can be used for divination as well as understand how information is communicated through the various senses. It includes step-by-step processes and activities to help you connect with your Spirit Guides, perceive and read information within the aura and chakra's as well as how to work with different divination tools such as tarot cards, pendulums and automatic writing for guidance into situations, events, relationships and possible opportunities for the future.

Mediumship Development: Connecting with Spirit

This book provides easy, simple and practical techniques you can use to understand more about how to blend and communicate with loved one's who have passed to Spirit through mediumship connections. You will also gain an understanding how to structure a sitting as well as how you can build a stronger relationship with your Spirit Guides to support you in your mediumship development. Included in this book you will find very simple strategies to help you understand the different types of evidence those in Spirit can bring through as well as fundamental skills necessary to deliver clear accurate evidential mediumship sittings to others.

ONE LAST THING...

If you enjoyed this book or found it useful, I would be very grateful if you can take a few moments to post a short review on Amazon. Your support really does make a difference and I read all the reviews personally so I can get your feedback and make this book even better.

If you'd like to leave a review then all you need to do is click the review link on this book's page on Amazon.

As a thank you for your support, I would love to invite you to kick off your shoes and join me in the **Barefoot Tribe** where you will receive channeled guidance from Spirit, gifts and more to support you on your journey. When you sign up you will also be the first to receive new episodes of Barefoot with Spirit podcast shows, details about up-coming webinars, events, masterclasses as well as early release and pre-sale on my products, services & offerings!

Sign-up via my website and I look forward to seeing you in the Tribe! Just remember ... **Shoes are absolutely optional!**

www.thebarefootmedium.com.au.

www.ingramcontent.com/pod-product-compliance
Lightning Source LLC
Chambersburg PA
CBHW051426090426
42737CB00014B/2852